T0327935

SOUK TO TABLE

Vibrant Middle Eastern Dishes for Everyday Meals

Amina Al-Saigh

ROCK POINT

© 2024 by Quarto Publishing Group USA, Inc.
Text and Photography © 2024 by Amina Al-Saigh

First published in 2024 by Rock Point, an imprint of The Quarto Group, 142 West 36th Street, 4th Floor, New York, NY 10018, USA
(212) 779-4972 www.Quarto.com

All rights reserved. No part of this book may be reproduced in any form without written permission of the copyright owners. All images in this book have been reproduced with the knowledge and prior consent of the artists concerned, and no responsibility is accepted by producer, publisher, or printer for any infringement of copyright or otherwise, arising from the contents of this publication. Every effort has been made to ensure the credits accurately comply with information supplied. We apologize for any inaccuracies that may have occurred and will resolve inaccurate or missing information in a subsequent reprinting of the book.

Rock Point titles are also available at discount for retail, wholesale, promotional and bulk purchase. For details, contact the Special Sales Manager by email at specialsales@quarto.com or by mail at The Quarto Group, Attn: Special Sales Manager, 100 Cummings Center Suite, 265D, Beverly, MA 01915, USA.

10 9 8 7 6 5 4 3 2

ISBN: 978-1-63106-976-5

Digital edition published in 2024
eISBN: 978-0-7603-8573-9

Publisher: Rage Kindelsperger
Editorial Director: Erin Canning
Creative Director: Laura Drew
Senior Art Director: Marisa Kwek
Managing Editor: Cara Donaldson
Cover & Interior Design: Georgie Hewitt

Printed in Bosnia & Herzegovina

To Mama and Baba: Your endless love and support have made this book possible. I will forever be grateful to you.

To Omar, Zayd, and Joud: Thank you for allowing me to test recipes on you. You are the light of my life.

Contents

Introduction

I wish I could start this introduction by saying that I am finally fulfilling my life-long dream of writing a cookbook. That ever since I was a little girl, I was in the kitchen, cooking and dreaming of one day sharing my food with the world. But that's not my story at all; in fact, the thought of writing a cookbook had never crossed my mind until well into my adult years. I was thrust into the online world of food by accident, and now, I find myself grateful to be part of it.

More specifically, I'm grateful to be able to bring you this cookbook that comes after years of perfecting

Middle Eastern cooking, reimagined through my lens. My passion for the last seven years has been to honor the rich tapestry of Middle Eastern flavors, while streamlining the process for today's fast-paced lifestyles. Each dish in this cookbook is a testament to my mission: to make the beloved flavors of my upbringing more accessible to the modern household and to redefine Middle Eastern food beyond just hummus and shawarma. In this cookbook, you will venture beyond the familiar realms of popularized dishes as I share the myriad bold and diverse recipes within everyday home cooking.

My hope is that this cookbook will ignite your love for this vibrant cuisine and get you excited about cooking dinner every day.

As for me and how I got here . . . Let me take you a few decades back, so we can make sense of why I am now sitting here, typing out the introduction to my first-ever cookbook.

Back to My Roots: My Iraq

I was born in Mosul, the second-largest city in Iraq, located in the north on the Tigris river. I only lived in Iraq for five short years before my parents decided to leave the country in 1995, in search of a brighter future for my sisters and me, since life in Iraq after the 1990 Gulf War was not looking bright. It was really my dad's ambition to leave. He was a chemistry professor at the University of Mosul, having earned his PhD in the UK. His life in the UK had opened his eyes to what life could be like outside of Iraq. Life in Iraq in the 1980s and early '90s, during the peak of the embargo and sanctions against Iraq, meant that people were earning lower salaries, not enough to feed a family. The basics of food necessities were controlled by the government and handed out in portions.

My dad continued to dream of leaving and finding a more prosperous place for him and my mother to raise their family. My mom was supportive but also apprehensive. The thought of leaving her family (most of whom remain in Iraq) and venturing out into the unknown worried her. But my mom was ambitious and dreamed of more for her family. Eventually, she agreed to leave. They packed up our life and off we went to spend the next five years living in Benghazi, Libya.

We did not leave Iraq because we had no love for it; on the contrary, we are proud Iraqis. We love our country, our culture, and our values. Iraq is the birthplace of many significant historical achievements that affect life around the world today, including the first human civilization in Mesopotamia. Aside from many significant inventions (like the wheel and mathematical and banking systems), the highlight of ancient Mesopotamian civilization was the reign of Hammurabi from 1792 to 1750 BCE, who was the first to develop a code of law in the lands.

Mesopotamia came under Arab influence in 636 CE. During the Abbasid Caliphate, beginning in the eighth century and lasting until the mid-thirteenth century, Baghdad became one of the greatest centers of civilization, a hub of economic trade routes. It was during this period that the first ever cookbook was written in Baghdad by Ibn Sayyar al-Warraq, called *Kitab al-Tabikh*, which translates to the "book of dishes." Due to its prosperity, the region drew people from all around the world, who brought their customs and recipes. Iraqi cuisine flourished—cooking was viewed as an art form to be pursued and perfected. Iraqis like my family have deep respect for food and tradition, many of us proud to represent our culture in diaspora.

I don't have any vivid memories of the first five years of my life in Iraq, but there are faint ones. I remember my grandmother's vast garden, full of trees, including an olive, lemon, plum, and orange tree, the smell of fruit wafting everywhere you went. Our life was full of family lunches and dinners, all of us cousins sitting on the floor, enjoying what my grandma cooked that day, always chanting in unison before eating: "Long live your hand, grandma!" Those who cook for us are deeply respected and cherished in Arab culture.

Iraqis (and Arabs in general) are known for their hospitality, so everyone was invited, and my mom, aunts, and grandmother would prepare large spreads of food—rice dishes topped with succulent lamb and jeweled with nuts and raisins, stuffed kibbeh dishes, stews and soups, and vibrant salads—followed by large spreads of desserts. In Iraq, the only way we know how to honor guests is to feed them. In Mosul, specifically, we are known to be excellent cooks, always making everything from scratch. I still remember when my father-in-law found out I was Moslawi, he told my now-husband, "You will be well fed."

When we left Iraq, my parents took with them what was deeply ingrained in their being: Iraqi culture, traditions, values, and pride, which were all passed down to my sisters and me.

My Upbringing in Canada

My childhood from the age of five to ten was spent in Benghazi, along the Mediterranean Sea. My fondest memories of that time include my sisters and me swimming for hours on end and then coming out of the water to be immediately enveloped by our mom's waiting arms. She would have jugs of fresh water ready to dump over us to wash away the salt and then wrap us up in towels and hand each of us a sandwich. They were either tuna, hard-boiled eggs, or cured meats—those were the best sandwiches I ever tasted.

Those five years will always hold a special place in my heart, but it was time for us to move on to our final destination: Canada. My parents applied to immigrate there, the paperwork fell into place, and off we went, saying goodbye to the warm weather and quickly learning to adjust to snow. I spent the next thirteen years of my life going to school, attending university for engineering, and enjoying what Canada had to offer with my family.

I can't speak for what life was like for my parents when they first arrived, or the years that followed, starting over, building a new life for their children. But from my perspective, I was young enough that the newness of it did not faze me. I jumped right into school, made friends, and was fortunate enough to fit right in. My family and I started to find a new identity as Arab Canadians, while still maintaining a firm grip onto our roots.

One of the easiest ways to hold onto our culture was through food. It was easy because . . . well, we simply could not stop eating our Iraqi food. My mom is the best cook I have known. Her palate is impeccable, her creativity and efficiency in the kitchen unmatched. My parents were both working hard to provide for us, but she always found time to make home-cooked meals. I remember walking home from school, excited to open the front door and sniff out what was for dinner that day. If it was a weekday, it would most likely be a lamb and vegetable stew, like okra or fasolia, with vermicelli rice, and those were my favorites. On weekends, my mom would make one of her grander dishes, like maqluba, biryani, or dolma.

Dinnertime was sacred for us; everyone had to be present. We sat together to eat and catch up as a family. After dinner, we would lounge around the living room, drinking chai and nibbling on salted nuts or sweet treats, watching an Arabic soap opera. This tradition never faltered, even as we grew older and busier. I remember my university years, when I would be overwhelmed with exams and assignments, but still made time for family chai.

On weekends and during celebrations, my mom would host friends and family, insisting that every single dish be cooked from scratch, by her. She would plan out the menus with my dad, who had a lot of input into the matter and acted as my mom's sous-chef. My dad loves food and is also a great cook. He would often saunter into the kitchen once the food was near completion and add a tiny pinch of salt to one dish, stir and sniff another one, or pour a bit of pomegranate molasses over the other, and then joke that his "final touches" made all the difference.

It wasn't just my parents who would cook; cooking and hosting were a family affair. My mom made sure to involve my sisters and me as much as she could, not just so we could learn to cook, but also to build our work ethic. We would divide the chores, with my youngest sister always choosing to stay outside of the kitchen and clean, while I was happiest doing kitchen tasks, most likely because of my dislike for cleaning over my love of food. I didn't think I loved to cook at the time, or maybe I didn't realize that I did, simply because I was focused on other goals. None of those goals involved cooking.

In fact, that is probably the last thing I thought I'd be doing, especially in my teenage years and early twenties. I was known in my family to be the one who planned to pursue a prestigious career and climb the corporate ladder. I used to watch my mom labor over our favorite Iraqi childhood dishes, such as dolma, coring all the vegetables, preparing the filling, and then meticulously filling each Swiss chard and grape leaf, rolling away and making two large pots at a time. I used to proudly exclaim, "I'm never going to do this when I have my own family. I'll just order pizza. Or I'll pay someone to cook for me."

These statements likely came because I was begrudgingly completing a task my mom had set for me, like peeling boiled almonds and slicing them in half for biryani (I highly suggest you buy peeled and sliced almonds). But I wasn't always disgruntled when helping my mom in the kitchen—it was probably only the days I thought I had something better to do. Looking back, those were some of the best years of my life. The fun we would have, the jokes and the laughter, the warmth that surrounded our family. Something must have registered deep in my brain, associating that love with food. But I still thought I wasn't going to turn into my mother in the kitchen.

I graduated from university with my chemical engineering degree, bright-eyed and ready to take on the world. I met my husband, Omar, in my last year of university. He was living in London and waiting for me to join him there. I got married, packed my bags, and moved to England. At the time, I was tearful at the thought of leaving the closest people to me. But looking back, spending five wonderful years in London with Omar was the best decision I'd ever made.

Finding Food as a Mother

In London, I embarked on my goal of a "prestigious career." I finished my master's degree and then started working for a company in the heart of the city. I enjoyed my years there, taking the train to work, coffee in hand, heels clicking as I switched platforms and made my way through the London hustle and bustle. My life was exactly what I wanted it to be. As a young engineer, I was a sponge, learning quickly and fortunate enough to cross paths with talented mentors who helped me shine in the corporate world.

Fast-forward three years and my son, Zayd, was born. I took a year-long maternity leave from my job and threw myself into motherhood. I enjoyed every minute of it. I'd take Zayd on walks through the parks of London and spend my days getting creative with cooking. I cooked a lot before Zayd was born as well; I loved making my husband's favorite foods. He had lived alone for so long, never learning how to cook. In fact, when I moved into his flat, he didn't even have salt in his cupboard. And when we went grocery shopping together for the first time, and I asked him to hand me a head of lettuce, he came back with a head of cabbage. That's what I was working with. Anything I made for him, he loved.

I had inherited my mom's palate, and although I had not yet learned some of her more complex dishes, I knew how to balance flavors. I found myself standing at the stove, tasting my stew, and all her tips and tricks would come to me, like adding a bit of acid to bring out the flavors, or knowing when the stew needed a pinch more salt, or letting it simply bubble away for twenty more minutes to concentrate the flavors. I slowly started to teach myself all my favorite childhood dishes, always calling her beforehand to go over the recipe together.

It was during my first maternity leave that my food blog was born. At the time, I was finding joy experimenting with food, and I decided to start an Instagram account and share my recipes with the world. When my maternity leave was over and I went back to work, life became busier. But the blog was my creative outlet, and I kept coming back to it.

I soon realized how much I loved flexing the creative muscles that weren't being used in my career. By day, I was crunching numbers and running multimillion-dollar engineering projects, and when I had free time, I was cooking and developing recipes. Slowly, a community started to build around the food I was sharing. It was mainly Middle Eastern food, but it was my way: easier, lighter, and quicker to fit into a busy lifestyle. I stayed true to my promise of not wanting to labor away in the kitchen, but I started to realize just how connected I was to my traditional food because of how my mom raised us. Food became my love language. It was how I wanted to teach my kids their culture. I realized that I absolutely was not going to order pizza every day, nor was I going to let anyone else cook for my family.

In 2018, we moved back to Canada, and I had my daughter, Joud. By this time, my food blog had grown substantially, and I continued dedicating time to it. I started to really listen to my audience and understand what they wanted: perfectly tested and accurate Middle Eastern recipes, with measurements, and tips on how to make them faster, easier. Because none of our Arab moms measured ingredients while cooking, they learned to cook with their senses. I became obsessed with sharing perfectly accurate recipes with helpful tips and tricks and hearing how they helped my readers. I received thousands of messages from my audience that touched my heart, and those are what kept me going.

At that time, my husband and I were both working full-time engineering jobs in Toronto (which meant long commutes in heavy traffic). After my maternity leave, I went back to a promotion at work. Suddenly, I was in management with a young team, working on a multitude of projects all while trying to juggle being a mother to two little children and keeping my blog afloat. This wasn't a bad thing at first. Being a leader at work was something I desired; I was excited and eager to prove myself. I had bright ideas, turned them into action, and saw my impact at work.

But over the span of two years, I realized that this new "life" I had was making me unhappy. I was working twelve-hour days, barely getting enough sleep. I was spending every weekend meal planning and doing chores, running errands, taking care of my kids, furiously switching from one task to another. I was unhappy with the corporate lifestyle: sitting for hours at my desk, taking call after call. Both my husband and I were burnt out.

In early 2023, I made the decision to quit my job. It was a monumental moment in my life: me—the girl who thought she'd be a CEO one day— quitting my ten-year career. At the time I made the decision, my publisher had contacted me about this cookbook. I considered it to be kismet. I threw myself into this project, as well as my blog, finally feeling like I could give it my full attention and continue to share my passion with my readers. I truly cherish the connection I have built with my online community. Knowing that my recipes are reaching your homes and bringing joy to your lives gives me purpose.

My Approach to Cooking

My approach to cooking is using the vibrant flavors and ingredients of Middle Eastern cuisine, but simplifying it for the modern, busy home cook. I love the authentic way of cooking the dishes I grew up eating.

But sometimes, there is an opportunity to make things lighter or easier—for example, roasting instead of frying vegetables, creating a one-pot version of a dish, or using appliances like an air fryer or pressure cooker to speed things up. Over time, I have found ways to make such changes but never jeopardize the flavor.

I also love cooking from across the region. The Middle East is not just one cuisine; it's large and multicultural. I love to showcase how varied the food can be by sharing my favorite dishes from countries such as Egypt, Lebanon, Syria, Palestine, Morocco, Libya, Turkey, Yemen, and Iran.

Aside from authentic flavors and recipes, I also love to experiment and develop recipes that aren't necessarily Middle Eastern but use Middle Eastern ingredients. This is what I think is truly unique about the collection of recipes in this cookbook: it's how I like to cook today—authentically Middle Eastern, from across the region, but made my way.

How To Use This Book

CONDIMENTS & DIPS

Use this section to make homemade condiments that will complement many of the recipes in the Main Dishes sections. Many of these condiments will keep in the refrigerator for at least a week, which means you'll have easy ways to amp up the flavor of lunch bowls and snacks. The dip recipes are a must for classic Middle Eastern mezze spreads if you are hosting or for easy snacking throughout the week.

SALADS & SIDES

My dinner table always has some sort of salad, most of the time my classic Salata (page 44) but also a few other favorites that will become staples. The sides include all kinds of rice recipes to serve alongside stews and proteins, because I have a thing for rice. But there are also other grains and vegetable sides and pastries that are perfect to round out your hosting table.

MAIN DISHES: 30 MINUTES & 1 HOUR

These are my favorite sections, with a promise that all thirty-two of these dinner-worthy recipes are bursting with flavor and quick and easy to make. There are a variety of dishes to keep dinnertime exciting for you and the family, including one-pot meals; chicken, seafood, and ground beef recipes; pastas; quick curries and stews; and easy casseroles.

MAIN DISHES: WORTH THE EFFORT

As an Arab, hosting is in my blood, and I absolutely love it! But even if I am not hosting, I love cooking special meals on the weekends. This is a collection of curated recipes that are my go-tos when I want to impress. They are not difficult to master; they just require a little more time. Some are a bit more hands-on, while others are only ten minutes of hands-on time with a lot of slow cooking in the oven. Flip through this section for your perfect lazy Sunday meal, or to plan your next get-together menu.

MAIN DISHES: SOUPS & STEWS

Comfort food is what I gravitate to, and growing up, stews were my favorite thing to eat. This section is full of hearty soups and stews that will warm and fill you up. The stews are vegetable focused and easy to make, while the soups offer the variety I love in the winter months.

DESSERTS & DRINKS

I am not a proficient baker, and for this reason precisely, I always find ways to make desserts that are easy but still impressive. This section includes my favorite must-make Middle Eastern desserts that show off the classic flavors of the cuisine. Serve these desserts alongside a hot drink like chai or Turkish coffee, or cold drinks in the summer months, for the perfect ending to every meal.

My Middle Eastern Pantry

In this section, I will walk you through all the ingredients typically found in my pantry and my fridge that are used quite often throughout the recipes in this book. The aim of this section is to help make your life easier with suggested substitutions. Thankfully, many specialty Middle Eastern ingredients are easily found in the international aisles of large supermarkets or at local Middle Eastern shops. I highly encourage you to seek out these ingredients because they will bring you closer to authentic Middle Eastern food. But just in case, this section will help you make any recipe in this book, even if you are missing a specialty ingredient.

Cooking Oils

EXTRA-VIRGIN OLIVE OIL

Extra-virgin olive oil is almost exclusively the only oil I use in my kitchen. The term "extra virgin" means that it is the highest grade of oil, produced by a simple cold-pressing process without the use of heat or chemicals. Olive oil has a robust fruity flavor with peppery notes, always adding more flavor to a dish rather than being neutral. When in doubt (and if you are cooking a savory dish), aside from deep frying, always reach for extra-virgin olive oil.

AVOCADO OIL

Avocado oil is what I reach for when I want a neutral, mild-flavored oil to use in any savory or sweet recipe. It is oil-pressed from the pulp of ripe avocados, rich in heart-healthy fats and antioxidants; it also has a high smoke point, making it great for high-temperature cooking. Whenever you see "vegetable oil" in a recipe, I highly recommend you use avocado oil as opposed to other highly processed seed oils.

Herbs & Spices

GROUND SPICES

It is essential to stock your pantry with high-quality spices in order to be able to recreate these Middle Eastern recipes easily. This spice section will help set you up to enjoy the variety of flavors and spice combinations without having to make a trip to the store every time. Middle Eastern cuisine uses many ground spices that are common across other cuisines and easy to find: cumin, coriander, cinnamon, paprika, cloves, onion powder, garlic powder, and cayenne pepper. Aside from these spices, here are several ground spices that are more characteristic of Middle Eastern cuisine and contribute to the unique flavors of the region.

SUMAC

Sumac is a vibrant and tangy spice made from crushed sumac berries that grow in the Mediterranean climate. It has a deep pink-red hue and a citrusy flavor profile that also has floral notes. It is often sprinkled on grilled meats or any oily food to brighten it with its tanginess. To substitute 1 teaspoon sumac, mix 2 teaspoons fresh lemon juice with 1 teaspoon grated lemon zest.

is not a blend of spices but rather comes from crushing allspice berries that grow in tropical climates. It was named "allspice" because those who first discovered it thought it tasted similar to a blend of cinnamon, cloves, and nutmeg. To substitute 1 teaspoon of allspice, mix ½ teaspoon ground cinnamon, ¼ teaspoon ground cloves, and ¼ teaspoon ground nutmeg.

TURMERIC (CURCUM)

Boasting a vibrant golden color and a mild and earthy flavor, turmeric is used in spice blends like curry powder, as well as in rice dishes, stews, and on meat, chicken, and fish. A little bit of turmeric goes a long way; adding too much of it can impart a bitter flavor. It is best to toast it in a bit of oil first to bring it to life and lose the bitterness. Turmeric can easily stain your hands, utensils, and counters, so be careful when using it!

SAFFRON (ZA'AFARAN)

The most expensive spice on Earth, saffron is luxurious not only because of its price but also due to its aroma and flavor. It is sold as threadlike red strands, imparting a delicate floral flavor with earthy and honey notes. One common mistake people make when using saffron is to throw in the strands as is, which does not extract the flavor correctly. Instead, crush the strands into a powder using a mortar and pestle, then bloom the saffron powder by adding a few tablespoons of hot water to it and allowing it to sit for 4 to 5 minutes. To substitute ½ teaspoon saffron, use ½ teaspoon turmeric to get the same golden hue you would get from saffron but not the flavor. It is hard to replicate saffron's unique flavor.

ALEPPO PEPPER (FILFIL HALABY)

Aleppo pepper is chili flakes made from a specific type of red peppers that come from the Syrian city of Aleppo. It is also known as *pul biber* in Turkey. It has a mild to moderate heat level that builds up slowly, along with earthy and citrusy notes. You may find it in stores as either sweet/mild or spicy; I always use the mild one. To substitute 1 teaspoon of Aleppo pepper, mix ¼ teaspoon cayenne pepper with ¾ teaspoon sweet paprika.

ALLSPICE (BHAR HELO)

If I was challenged to pick a favorite spice, it would be allspice. Allspice

CARDAMOM (HEIL)

A key and prized ingredient, cardamom is used in savory and sweet dishes, as well as infused in hot drinks like tea and coffee. The green variety is the one used most often. Cardamom adds depth and sophistication to rice dishes, meats, and stews. You'll never catch an Arab boiling lamb without using a few cardamom pods to impart a pleasant fragrance over any gamey smell. It is used both whole (pods) and ground.

DRIED LIME (NOOMI BASRA OR LOOMI)

One of the most unique flavors used in Middle Eastern cuisine, specifically in Iraq and the Persian Gulf countries, is dried lime. Limes are dried in the sun until they become dark and brittle and then used either whole or ground. Dried limes have a subdued tangy flavor, with deep earthy and slightly bitter notes. When used as part of a seasoning mix, they are ground (without the seeds) into a powder. When used in stews and soups, they are kept whole and pricked with a knife a few times to allow cooking juices to penetrate them. I find it easier to submerge them in hot water for a few minutes first to soften, and then I use a pointed knife to pierce them in three places. There is no direct substitute for dried limes, but to get a bit closer to the flavor, try using 1 tablespoon lime juice and 1 teaspoon grated lime zest for each dried lime.

CURRY POWDER (KARI)

A yellow blend of many spices, curry powder is used widely across Iraq, where it is also known as *bahar asfar*, which means "yellow spice mix." It was brought over as the creation of British cooks in their attempt to emulate Indian curry dishes. It is found in both mild and spicy varieties. To substitute 2 teaspoons curry powder, mix ½ teaspoon ground cumin, ½ teaspoon ground coriander, ¼ teaspoon ground turmeric, ¼ teaspoon ground ginger, ¼ teaspoon ground fenugreek, and ¼ teaspoon ground black pepper.

BAHARAT

The term *baharat* in Arabic is used to refer to a spice blend, with each household having its own favorite blend. Although there is no one correct recipe for baharat, most versions are similar to the Indian garam masala, which makes a great substitute. You can find the recipe for my mom's Baharat on page 122 which makes 6½ teaspoons. Use this mixture as an easy boost of flavor in rice dishes, stews, and as part of marinades for meats, chicken, or fish.

SEVEN SPICE

Seven spice is the Levant region's version of baharat, consisting of seven warm spices and also sometimes referred to as *baharat*. The following is a great recipe to make your own mix and then adjust the ratios to your liking. In a pinch, you can also resort to using allspice. The following recipe makes roughly 3 tablespoons. Mix 2 teaspoons ground allspice, 2 teaspoons ground coriander, 2 teaspoons ground cinnamon, 1 teaspoon ground cumin, 1 teaspoon ground cloves, 1 teaspoon ground nutmeg, and 1 teaspoon black pepper.

ZA'ATAR

Za'atar is perhaps one of the most well-known Middle Eastern herb and spice blends, due to its unique flavor profile and texture. It is a blend native to the Levantine region of Lebanon, Palestine, Syria, and Jordan, with each region having a unique variation. It includes toasted sesame seeds, sumac, and dried wild oregano native to the region, with some variations also adding cumin and/or caraway. Za'atar is usually enjoyed as a dip with olive oil, and it also makes an amazing marinade for meats, chicken, and fish, as well as on roasted vegetables or mixed into salad dressings. Make sure you find high-quality za'atar, as many lower-quality brands tend to use wheat fillers and citric acid in place of sumac. To make your own za'atar, mix 1 tablespoon dried oregano, 1 tablespoon dried thyme, 1 tablespoon sumac, and 2 tablespoons toasted sesame seeds. Use high-quality ingredients for best results.

WHOLE SPICES

Whole spices are used to flavor meat stews and tossed into aromatic rice dishes. They impart their flavor slowly but season the meat from within, transforming the flavor over time. They are best used in slow-simmered recipes to allow them time to penetrate and release their fragrance. The most important way to use them is in meat and chicken broths and stews, especially with lamb, in order to enhance the flavor and mask any "gaminess". Here are the essential whole spices I use when making stews and broths: green cardamom pods, cinnamon sticks, and bay leaves. I also throw in the following optional but recommended spices: cloves, allspice berries, and black peppercorns.

SALT & BLACK PEPPER

All the recipes in this cookbook were tested using kosher salt. Kosher salt is a pure salt that does not contain iodine or anticaking agents. It is coarse and its crystals are larger than table salt. It's ideal for seasoning with your fingertips while you cook. I specify the amount of salt in teaspoons for each recipe, along with when it should be added. I do this because it is extremely essential to season food with salt correctly; often, an extra pinch of salt can take a dish from boring to vibrant, and it is a skill that is built over time. If you only buy table salt or other types of salt, don't feel the need to switch to kosher salt to make these recipes. Simply use this conversion as a start and then adjust to your taste:

1¼ teaspoons kosher salt – 1 teaspoon table salt = 1 teaspoon fine sea salt = 1 teaspoon fine pink Himalayan salt

As for black pepper, I alternate between freshly cracked black pepper when my pepper mill is full and store-bought ground pepper when I can't be bothered to refill my pepper mill. Black pepper is always to your taste.

Nuts, Grains, & Legumes

RICE (ROZ)

Long-grain basmati rice is the standard rice I use in most of my rice dishes, simply due to its flavor and ease to cook. It is one of the "sturdier" types of rice, standing up to moisture quite well, which means it is hard to mess it up. I typically use a 1:1.5 ratio of rice to liquid, though some varieties may need a bit more liquid, so a 1:2 ratio may also work (you will need to experiment with your favorite brand). Another common type of rice I use is Egyptian rice, which is a medium-grain rice. Medium-grain rice needs a 1:1 ratio of rice to liquid if cooking it as a pilaf, with a thirty-minute presoak to cook up to fluffy perfection.

BULGUR WHEAT (BURGHOL)

Bulgur, also referred to as cracked wheat, is an essential grain used in many Middle Eastern recipes. It comes in coarse, medium, and fine varieties. Fine bulgur is used in tabbouleh and does not need to be cooked but simply soaked in salad juices. Coarse bulgur is cooked the same way as rice and takes about 30 minutes to make. Bulgur boasts a nutty flavor, packed with much more fiber than rice.

FREEKEH

Freekeh is a nutritious, ancient whole grain made from green, young wheat that's harvested early. It has a chewy texture and a nutty, smoky flavor, because the freekeh grains are fire-roasted when prepared. It is commonly used in soups and salads and as a stuffing for chicken and vegetables.

COUSCOUS

While couscous looks and acts like a grain, it is tiny specks of pasta made from semolina flour. It is the main "grain" used in the North African countries of Morocco, Tunisia, Algeria, and Libya. I love it because it does not need to be cooked; simply soak it in chicken broth using a 1:1 ratio and cover it for five minutes. Then I like to fluff it with a fork, drizzle it with some olive oil, and add freshly chopped herbs, toasted nuts, or spices.

SEMOLINA (SAMEED)

Semolina is a flour made from durum wheat. It is yellowish in color and similar to cornmeal in its gritty texture. It comes in either fine, medium, or coarse grind and is often used in desserts.

VERMICELLI NOODLES (SHA'ARIYA)

This is a type of pasta commonly cooked with white rice to create a noodle and rice dish (Roz Bi Shaariya on page 67) that every Arab household makes and serves with stews. The vermicelli noodles are sold either broken into ½-inch (13 mm) thin noodle pieces or as nests that you crush by hand before cooking. The noodles are toasted in oil until deeply golden and then cooked with rice.

Specialty Ingredients

POMEGRANATE MOLASSES (DIBS RUMMAN)

If I were to pick just one ingredient to urge you to buy, use, and love, it would be pomegranate molasses. It is made by simmering and reducing pomegranate juice, often adding a little bit of lemon juice and sugar to amp up the natural tartness and sweetness of the fruit. As an Iraqi, I am genetically disposed to love the sweet-and-sour flavor profile in savory dishes, so pomegranate molasses is my best friend in the kitchen. Just a tablespoon or two of this ingredient added to stews, salad dressings, and meat marinades and drizzled over roasted vegetables will take your dish to another level. It is quite easy to find in the international aisle of your supermarket, but you can also make it at home. Here's an easy method to make 1 cup (240 ml):

1. Place 4 cups (1 quart, or 1 L) pomegranate juice in a medium saucepan. You can use bottled pure pomegranate juice, or remove the seeds from 8 large pomegranates, roughly blend them in a blender, and then strain through a fine-mesh sieve to end up with only juice.

2. Add ¼ cup (60 ml) fresh lemon juice and ⅓ cup plus 1 tablespoon (70 g) granulated sugar to the pan and stir. Let the mixture come to a simmer over low heat. (Do not bring it to a rapid boil, or you risk it not tasting as good, almost as if it is too "cooked.") Keep the mixture at a low simmer for 2 hours or more, stirring occasionally, until it has reduced to a thick syrup that easily coats the back of a spoon.

3. Allow it to cool then store it in an airtight jar in the fridge. It should last months.

LABNEH

Labneh is a creamy thickened yogurt that resembles the texture of cream cheese. It is a common Middle Eastern dairy product usually consumed for breakfast. Smear some labneh over a large piece of pita bread, sprinkle it with za'atar, and top with fresh cucumbers, tomatoes, and mint leaves and then roll and enjoy it like a sandwich.

TAHINI (TAHINA)

Tahini is a Middle Eastern staple, and my cupboard is never without a large jar. Tahini is made by grinding toasted sesame seeds into a paste. It is deeply nutty and silky in texture, adding depth to dishes it is used in. Growing up in Iraq, we typically have it for breakfast, drizzling it with date molasses and dipping bread into it. It's our version of peanut butter and jam. High-quality tahini is always made from toasted sesame seeds, never bitter, and smooth in texture after mixing, since the oil tends to separate. If you can't get your hands on a jar of high-quality tahini, you can make it at home. Here's an easy method to make 1 cup (240 ml):

1. In a small pan over low heat, toast 1⅓ cups (200 g) of sesame seeds, stirring constantly, until fragrant and lightly golden, 3 to 4 minutes.

2. Transfer the toasted sesame seeds to a small, powerful food processor and process for 1 to 2 minutes until the seeds are ground. Add 2 to 3 tablespoons of neutral vegetable oil (such as avocado oil) and continue processing until a smooth paste forms. This should take about 5 minutes depending on the processor's power.

3. Transfer to an airtight mason jar and store at room temperature for a few months.

RED PEPPER PASTE (BIBER SALCASI)

Red pepper paste is a staple Turkish condiment, made from seeded red peppers that are crushed with salt and then left out in the sun to dry and concentrate in flavor. The result is a thick paste resembling the look and texture of tomato paste. It comes in two varieties: hot (*aci*) and sweet (*tatli*). I tend to always buy the sweet variety and use it to amp up the flavor of rice dishes, soups, stews, and marinades.

ROSE WATER (MAY WARID) & ORANGE BLOSSOM WATER (MAZAHER)

The flavor and aroma of rose is always reminiscent of Middle Eastern desserts, as it is used abundantly to add subtle floral notes and a luxurious aroma. A bottle of rose water will last quite a while in your cupboard and using very little will go a long way. Orange blossom water is used in the same way, often with rose water or as a substitute for it.

Condiments & Dips

Toum

GARLIC SAUCE

YIELD: 2 cups (480 ml)

PREP TIME: 10 minutes

◇◇◇◇◇

1 cup (155 g) cloves garlic, peeled (pre-peeled works as long as they are fresh)

½ cup (120 ml) fresh lemon juice

2 teaspoons kosher salt

2 cups (480 ml) neutral oil (such as avocado oil)

Toum is an Arabic word that translates to "garlic." This addictive sauce comes from the Levantine region and has made its way across not just the Middle East, but most of the Western world. Simply put: you cannot have a shawarma without first smearing spoonfuls of this sauce on your bread. You can make it using an immersion blender or a food processor. When I have a large jar of toum in my fridge, it also makes its way into chicken or meat marinades, salad dressings, and dipping—basically, any recipe that uses the combination of garlic and oil!

1 Cut the garlic cloves in half lengthwise and remove the green germ if necessary. (The germ will make the toum bitter.)

2 In a tall jug or jar that fits an immersion blender, place the garlic, lemon juice, and salt and blend until a paste forms and develops some foam, 20 to 30 seconds, depending on the power of your blender.

3 While the blender is still inside the container, add the oil. Start blending, keeping the blades at the bottom of the jar and slowly pulsing it up and down slightly. Do this for 3 to 5 minutes, until the oil and the garlic start to emulsify. (The emulsification will slowly work its way up the jar until the whole sauce is emulsified; see Notes.)

4 Store in an airtight jar in the refrigerator for 3 to 4 weeks.

Notes

+ You can also make toum using a food processor. If you have a 7- or 9-cup (1.7 or 2.1 L) food processor, I recommend using the smaller insert that some machines come with; otherwise, you will need to double this recipe. The garlic will not puree properly in a bowl that's too large. Simply puree the garlic with the salt, then, with the food processor running, slowly add the oil and lemon juice, alternating them, and ensuring that the last liquid you add in is the oil.

+ If the toum does not emulsify, you can fix it by adding the whites of 1 egg to the jar and continue blending. If you add an egg white, use the sauce within 1 to 2 days.

Tunisian Harissa
CHILI PASTE

YIELD: 2 cups (370 g)

PREP TIME: 25 minutes

◇◇◇◇◇

¾ ounce (21 g) dried chili peppers (such as guajillo, Kashmiri, or any other pepper), sliced lengthwise and seeds and stems removed

1½ teaspoons caraway seeds

1½ teaspoons cumin seeds

1½ teaspoons coriander seeds

6½ ounces (180 g) jarred roasted red peppers

1 cup (50 g) sun-dried tomatoes

4 large cloves garlic, peeled

1 teaspoon kosher salt, plus more if needed

2 tablespoons fresh lemon juice

2 teaspoons grated lemon zest

¼ cup (60 ml) olive oil, plus more for topping

Harissa is a Tunisian chili paste that is traditionally made with rehydrated dried chili peppers pureed with olive oil, garlic, and a mix of spices. I went to a Tunisian primary school, and I have vivid memories of my sister and I treating ourselves to "tin hareesa" sandwiches, a soft bun smeared with harissa and filled with canned tuna. Looking back now, I'm not sure how eight-year-old me was able to handle the spice level. Nowadays, I like a slightly milder harissa, which is why I love adding roasted red peppers and sun-dried tomatoes. Neither are traditional additions, but they help to amp up the umami and tone down the spice level a bit. Use this recipe in marinades, add spoonfuls of it to stews and soups, smear it on sandwiches, and make harissa mayonnaise.

1 Bring water to a boil in a kettle or pot.

2 Place the chili peppers in a medium bowl and submerge them in boiling water. Cover with foil or a lid and let sit for 15 minutes.

3 In a small, dry skillet, toast the caraway, cumin, and coriander seeds over low heat for 2 minutes, or until fragrant, stirring continuously. Transfer the toasted seeds to a mortar and pestle or a spice grinder and grind into a powder (see Note).

4 Drain the chili peppers and gently pat them and the red peppers dry. Add the chilies, ground seeds, red peppers, sun-dried tomatoes, garlic, salt, lemon juice, lemon zest, and oil to a small food processor and process until a smooth paste forms. Taste and adjust for more salt if needed. (If you prefer it spicier, add more chili peppers.)

5 Transfer the harissa to a 2-cup (480 ml) container with an airtight lid. Cover the top with an even layer of oil, seal the lid, and store in the refrigerator and use within 2 to 3 weeks. Always use a clean utensil when serving and replenish the olive oil layer with each use.

Note

If you don't have a mortar and pestle or spice grinder, you can use ground spices instead—only 1 teaspoon of each spice, because they are more concentrated.

Moroccan Chermoula

YIELD: 1½ cups (360 g)

PREP TIME: 10 minutes

◇◇◇◇◇

2 cups (100 g) packed roughly
chopped fresh parsley (about
1 bunch)

1 cup (40 g) packed roughly chopped
fresh cilantro (about ½ bunch)

2 large cloves garlic, crushed

1 teaspoon paprika

1 teaspoon ground cumin

1 teaspoon ground coriander

½ teaspoon kosher salt

½ teaspoon cayenne pepper, or more
to taste

½ cup (120 ml) olive oil

3 tablespoons fresh lemon juice

1 teaspoon grated lemon zest

There's nothing that elevates a steak or grilled chicken dish quite like a zingy and herby chermoula. Chermoula is a North African condiment used across Morocco, Tunisia, Libya, and Algeria. It is similar to the Latin American chimichurri but distinguished by spices like cumin, coriander, and paprika, which turn it into more of a brownish-green sauce instead of bright green. It's made slightly differently across these countries, with Libyan chermoula being very different, resembling more of a cucumber and tomato salad rather than a sauce. This recipe is closest to the Moroccan version, with parsley and cilantro forming the green backbone of the sauce. And if you're not faint-hearted, feel free to kick up the heat by adding more cayenne (I'm still working on my heat tolerance). My favorite way to use chermoula is in Chermoula Meatballs (page 96).

1 Add the parsley, cilantro, and garlic to a small food processor and pulse until finely chopped.

2 Add the paprika, cumin, coriander, salt, cayenne, oil, lemon juice, and lemon zest and pulse a few more times to combine. The sauce texture should be rough, not smooth.

3 Store in an airtight container in the refrigerator and use within 1 to 2 weeks.

Labneh

YIELD: 1¾ cups (380 g)

PREP TIME: 10 minutes, plus 24 hours straining

◇◇◇◇◇

LABNEH

3 cups (720 ml) plain, whole-milk yogurt (6% to 11% fat)

1 teaspoon kosher salt

TOPPINGS (OPTIONAL)

Olive oil

Za'atar

Garlic

Chili flakes

Olives

Fresh herbs

FOR SERVING

Pita bread

If you see the refrigerator light on at midnight, I am likely standing there with the door open, pita bread in hand, scooping up labneh as my midnight snack of choice. It's too hard to resist and so easy to eat. Labneh (pronounced "lab-naa" in other Arabic dialects) is tangy and creamy strained yogurt, resembling the texture of cream cheese. It's surprisingly easy to make at home; just mix yogurt with salt and strain it! But this simple process, typically done using a cheesecloth, allows all the whey to drain away, leaving behind a thicker and creamier product. The most traditional way of enjoying labneh is spread onto a plate, drizzled generously with olive oil, and sprinkled with za'atar. But I also love spooning it into warm cooked pasta for my picky six-year-old or using it as a canvas for grilled or roasted veggies (see Roasted Eggplant with Labneh on page 83). Make sure you don't discard the protein-rich whey left behind; throw it into a smoothie or a bowl of oatmeal.

1 In a medium bowl, mix together the yogurt and salt. (You can also add the salt directly to the yogurt tub to avoid dirtying another dish.)

2 In a separate medium bowl, place a fine-mesh strainer so that it is elevated and not touching the bottom of the bowl. Line the strainer with a cheesecloth. (If you do not have a cheesecloth, layer thick paper towels in the strainer instead.)

3 Transfer the yogurt into the cheesecloth and lift all corners of the cloth to tie it into a secure knot. (You can also rest a wooden spoon at the top of the bowl and tie the cheesecloth to the spoon with a trivet underneath to ensure it does not touch the bottom of the bowl.) Allow it to strain for 24 hours in the refrigerator, or up to 48 hours for an even thicker consistency.

4 Spread the labneh onto a plate and top with olive oil and your preferred toppings. Serve with pita bread.

Note

To make a garlic, mint, and walnut labneh dip, combine 1½ cups (350 g) of labneh, 1½ teaspooons of dried mint, 1 small, crushed garlic clove, ¼ teaspoon of kosher salt, and ¾ ounce (20 g) of unsalted chopped raw walnuts. Mix all the ingredients and serve in a bowl garnished with olive oil and more dried mint.

Tarator
TAHINI SAUCE

YIELD: 1 cup (240 ml)
PREP TIME: 10 minutes

◇◇◇◇◇

1 cup (240 ml) tahini
1 large clove garlic, crushed
¼ cup (60 ml) fresh lemon juice
1 teaspoon kosher salt
⅛ teaspoon black pepper, or more
   to taste

FOR GARNISHING
2 tablespoons roughly chopped
   fresh parsley

This is probably the most common sauce you'll find in the Middle East, usually referred to as *tarator*. This tahini sauce is drizzled on wraps, salads, and grilled vegetables, and more specifically, it is always drizzled on falafel and beef shawarma wraps. To make it, all you need is high-quality tahini paste, lemon juice, and crushed garlic. Whisk them together and season with salt and pepper and some water, and you're ready to drizzle. It's very nutty and lemony and will brighten up anything you add it to.

1 Add the tahini and crushed garlic to a medium bowl and whisk to combine.

2 Slowly add the lemon juice and whisk; the mixture will start to seize up and look very dry.

3 Gradually add about ¾ cup (180 ml) of water, 2 to 3 tablespoons at a time, while whisking until the mixture is smooth.

4 Season with the salt and pepper and garnish with the chopped parsley.

Note
Drizzle this sauce on salads and sandwiches or use as a dipping sauce. Store in an airtight jar in the refrigerator for up to 1 week. You may need to loosen the tarator slightly with water when using it again.

Egyptian Dukkah
NUT & SEED SPICE BLEND

YIELD: ½ cup (65 g)
PREP TIME: 10 minutes
COOK TIME: 5 minutes

◇◇◇◇◇

1 teaspoon cumin seeds
1 teaspoon coriander seeds
3 tablespoons sesame seeds
3 tablespoons chopped pistachios
2 tablespoons chopped hazelnuts
½ teaspoon kosher salt
¼ teaspoon cayenne pepper, or more to taste

Dukkah is a condiment or spice blend that is commonly made in Egyptian households. Each family has its own unique blend, but the most common components are nuts, sesame seeds, and warm spices like coriander and cumin, which are toasted to intensify their flavor and then ground into a coarse mixture using a mortar and pestle. Dukkah will quite easily transform anything it is sprinkled on. Egyptians enjoy it simply by dipping a piece of bread in olive oil and then into the dukkah. But it is also used to season fish, chicken, and meats, as well as grilled vegetables, dips, and salads. Make a batch of dukkah and keep it in a tightly covered jar on your counter. You're sure to find creative ways to use it throughout the week. One of my favorites is in Roasted Dukkah-Crusted Trout (page 152). You can also mix it with olive oil and use it as a dipping sauce or slather the spiced oil onto pita breads and crisp them up for dukkah-spiced pita chips.

1 Place a small, dry skillet over medium heat and add the cumin and coriander. Toast for a few minutes, or until fragrant and slightly darker in color, stirring continuously. Transfer to a spice grinder or mortar and pestle. Toast the sesame seeds the same way, reserve 1 tablespoon, and add the rest to the spice grinder or mortar and pestle. Grind to a fine powder and place in a small bowl.

2 Add the pistachios and hazelnuts to the same skillet and toast over medium heat for a few minutes, or until fragrant, stirring often. Transfer the toasted nuts to a spice grinder and pulse a few times, maintaining a coarse texture. Add them to the bowl with the ground seeds.

3 Add the salt, cayenne, and reserved sesame seeds to the bowl with the seeds and nuts and mix well.

4 Store in an airtight container at room temperature and use within a few days.

Note
Sprinkle dukkah on hummus, eggs, labneh, avocado toast, and even popcorn. Use as seasoning in salad dressings, toss with roasted vegetables, and rub on meat, chicken, and fish.

Hummus with Beef

YIELD: 4 cups (1 kg); 6 to 8 servings

PREP TIME: 10 minutes

COOK TIME: 15 minutes

◇◇◇◇◇

HUMMUS

2 large cloves garlic

¼ cup (60 ml) fresh lemon juice, plus more if needed

3 tablespoons olive oil

1 teaspoon kosher salt, plus more if needed

36 ounces (1 kg) canned chickpeas, drained and ¾ cup (180 ml) of the liquid (aquafaba) reserved

½ cup (120 ml) tahini

2 ice cubes

BEEF

18 ounces (500 g) boneless steak (ribeye, sirloin, or flank), cut into bite-size pieces

1 teaspoon kosher salt

½ teaspoon black pepper

½ teaspoon ground allspice

1 tablespoon unsalted butter or ghee

¼ cup pine nuts (30 g) or slivered almonds (35 g)

FOR GARNISHING AND SERVING

¼ cup (13 g) finely chopped parsley

¼ cup (50 g) pomegranate arils (optional)

Olive oil

Pita bread

Hummus is likely the gateway to Middle Eastern cuisine for many people. This chickpea and tahini dip needs no introduction, and you'll likely find a tub of it at every supermarket. But let me state this: homemade hummus is always much better than anything you can buy, even if you follow my quick method below using canned chickpeas. You can make it extra lemony, or extra garlicky. My absolute favorite way to enjoy it is with seasoned and caramelized steak on top, which not only turns it into a satisfying meal but will also have you addicted. You can use ground beef or even throw leftover shawarma on top, as many restaurants do.

1 TO MAKE THE HUMMUS: Add the garlic, lemon juice, and oil to a food processor and process for a few seconds until combined. Add the salt, chickpeas, and tahini to the food processor and process for a few minutes, or until the hummus starts to come together. Add the ice cubes while the food processor is running and slowly drizzle in the reserved chickpea liquid. Process the mixture for at least 5 minutes to yield a creamy texture. Taste and adjust for more salt and lemon juice if needed. Place in the refrigerator to cool for a few minutes.

2 MEANWHILE, MAKE THE BEEF: Season the steak pieces with the salt, pepper, and allspice.

3 In a large cast-iron skillet, melt the butter over medium-high heat. Add the meat and cook for 5 to 7 minutes, until caramelized, working in batches to avoid overcrowding. Remove the beef from the pan.

4 Add the pine nuts to the same skillet and lightly toast them over low heat for 3 to 5 minutes, until golden, stirring continuously.

5 Assemble by spreading the hummus on a plate, topping with some of the beef and pine nuts, and garnishing with the parsley, pomegranate arils (if using), and a drizzle of oil. Serve with pita bread.

Baba Ghanoush
SMOKED EGGPLANT DIP

YIELD: 2 cups (470 g); 6 servings

PREP TIME: 10 minutes

COOK TIME: 45 minutes

◇◇◇◇◇

2 large eggplants (1 to 1⅓ pounds, or 500 to 600 g, each)

½ cup (120 ml) tahini

½ to 1 teaspoon kosher salt, or more to taste

¼ teaspoon black pepper

1 small clove garlic, crushed

3 to 4 tablespoons fresh lemon juice, or more to taste

FOR GARNISHING AND SERVING

¼ cup (35 g) pine nuts

Olive oil

Pomegranate arils (optional)

Finely chopped fresh parsley (optional)

The name of this smoked eggplant dip has stumped many of us Arabs. When translated literally, the word *baba* means "daddy," and the word *ghanoush* means "spoiled" or "indulged." Put them together and you have "spoiled daddy," which does very little to describe what this dip is. But, odd name aside, this dip has gained almost as much popularity as hummus, with its creamy texture and slightly smoked eggplant flavor. The eggplants are typically roasted on an open flame, either a gas stove or a grill. The charred skin is then peeled, and the soft flesh is scooped out and mixed with tahini, lemon juice, garlic, and seasoning. Many variations also add a bit of yogurt to the mix for extra creaminess and tartness. This is a dip that really doesn't need precise measurements. You start adding your ingredients, mixing them up and tasting and adjusting until you reach your perfect flavor.

1 Preheat the oven to 450°F (230°C). Line a large baking sheet with aluminum foil.

2 Pierce the eggplants with a knife to create 4 or 5 slits all over; this helps the steam to escape.

3 If you have a gas stove, use tongs to char each eggplant's skin all over on an open flame, rotating them carefully for a few minutes until the skin is blistered. If you have an electric or induction stove, you can char the eggplants' skin in a hot cast-iron skillet without any oil. Rotate the eggplants for a few minutes until the skin is blistered, then proceed to baking.

4 Place the eggplants on the prepared baking sheet and bake for 45 minutes, or until they are soft and can be easily pierced with a fork.

5 Cut the eggplants in half lengthwise and scoop out the flesh using a fork or spoon. Place the flesh in a fine-mesh strainer over a small bowl and allow it to drain its liquid for a few minutes.

6 Transfer the drained flesh to a medium bowl with the tahini, salt, pepper, garlic, and lemon juice. Mash it using a fork; this will create a chunky consistency. (If you like it smooth, you can pulse it in a food processor or use an immersion blender.) Adjust the seasoning to your liking.

7 Toast the pine nuts in a small, dry skillet over medium heat, for 5 minutes, or until golden, stirring continuously.

8 Serve the baba ghanoush topped with oil, toasted pine nuts, pomegranate arils (if using), and parsley (if using).

Syrian Muhammara
ROASTED RED PEPPER & WALNUT DIP

YIELD: 2¼ cups (520 g); 6 servings
PREP TIME: 10 minutes
COOK TIME: 35 minutes

◇◇◇◇◇

3 large red bell peppers, cut in half and seeds and stems removed (or use 10½ ounces, or 300 g, jarred roasted red peppers; see Note)

½ cup (50 g) bread crumbs

½ cup (50 g) unsalted whole raw walnuts

2 tablespoons pomegranate molasses

¼ cup (60 ml) olive oil

1 large clove garlic

1 teaspoon ground Aleppo pepper (or substitute with ½ teaspoon chili flakes)

½ teaspoon kosher salt

4 small sun-dried tomatoes

1 tablespoon tomato paste

1 tablespoon fresh lemon juice

FOR GARNISHING AND SERVING
Pomegranate molasses
Unsalted chopped raw walnuts
Finely chopped fresh parsley
Pita bread

Note

If you are using jarred roasted red peppers, they are already roasted, so you can skip to step 5.

Muhammara is an iconic Syrian mezze dip made primarily from roasted red peppers and walnuts. I find that it's lesser known in the Western world but quite possibly one of the most delicious dips you'll try. It is rich, sweet, tart, and slightly smoky, with a thick, spreadable consistency. It's known for its vibrant red color, which is why it is called *muhammara*, meaning "reddened" in Arabic. Many versions will use bread crumbs to thicken the dip, as well as tomato paste for redness. I love to add a nontraditional ingredient to my recipe: sun-dried tomatoes. I find they add a concentrated and robust flavor, amping up the umami and sweetness. Make this dip ahead of time and store it in the fridge up to a week.

1 Preheat the oven to 450°F (230°C).

2 Place the peppers, skin sides down, in a large cast-iron pan over medium-high heat and char for 5 to 6 minutes, until the skins are blistered.

3 Cover the pan with aluminum foil and bake for 30 to 45 minutes, until the peppers are soft. Remove from the oven and let rest, still covered, for 10 minutes; this helps them to soften and makes removing the skins easier.

4 Carefully peel the peppers with tongs or your hands and discard the skins.

5 Lightly toast the bread crumbs in a medium, dry skillet over medium heat for 3 to 5 minutes, until they are slightly darker in color, stirring continuously, then remove from the pan.

6 Lightly toast the walnuts in the same skillet over medium heat for 3 to 5 minutes, until slightly darker and fragrant, stirring continuously, then remove from the pan.

7 Add the roasted peppers, toasted bread crumbs, toasted walnuts, pomegranate molasses, oil, garlic, Aleppo pepper, salt, sun-dried tomatoes, tomato paste, and lemon juice to a food processor. Process until a paste forms, stopping to scrape down the sides of the food processor as necessary. The final dip should be a bit lumpy.

8 Spread the muhammara onto a dish and garnish with pomegranate molasses, walnuts, and parsley. Serve with pita bread.

Musabaha

MASHED CHICKPEAS & TAHINI

YIELD: 2½ cups (570 g); 6 servings

PREP TIME: 10 minutes

COOK TIME: 10 minutes

◇◇◇◇◇

18 ounces (510 g) chickpeas, drained and half the liquid (aquafaba) reserved

2 large cloves garlic, crushed

¾ teaspoon kosher salt, plus more if needed

½ teaspoon ground cumin

¼ cup (60 ml) fresh lemon juice

½ cup (120 ml) tahini

FOR GARNISHING AND SERVING

¼ cup (13 g) finely chopped fresh parsley

½ teaspoon paprika

Olive oil

Pita bread

If you love hummus and a chunky texture, then you'll love musabaha. It is another classic Levantine dip, very similar to hummus, but with one main difference: the chickpeas are left whole or slightly mashed. It's also more heavily seasoned with cumin and paprika.

1 Place the chickpeas and the reserved aquafaba in a medium saucepan over medium heat. Add 1 cup (240 ml) of water to cover the chickpeas, bring to a boil, and boil for 5 to 7 minutes.

2 In a medium bowl, combine the garlic, salt, cumin, and lemon juice.

3 Using a slotted spoon, remove all the hot chickpeas from the saucepan, reserving a few tablespoons for garnish, and place the rest of the chickpeas in the bowl with the lemon juice and garlic. Add ¼ cup (60 ml) of the boiling water from the saucepan to the bowl. Mix everything together, then add the tahini and continue to mix. As you are mixing, mash some of the chickpeas but leave most of them whole. If required, add a few more tablespoons of the chickpea cooking liquid to loosen the sauce. Taste and adjust for more salt if needed.

4 Spoon the musabaha into a serving bowl and garnish with the chopped parsley, paprika, oil, and reserved chickpeas. Serve with pita bread.

Salads & Sides

Salata

EVERYDAY CHOPPED SALAD

YIELD: 4 servings

PREP TIME: 15 minutes

◇◇◇◇◇

SALATA

4 small Persian cucumbers, small diced

1 large tomato, small diced

½ small red onion, small diced

1 medium bell pepper (any color), small diced

½ cup (25 g) finely chopped fresh parsley

¼ teaspoon kosher salt

DRESSING

½ cup (120 ml) olive oil

½ cup (120 ml) fresh lemon juice

2 tablespoons pomegranate molasses

1 teaspoon sumac

1 teaspoon dried mint

½ teaspoon kosher salt

FOR GARNISHING

Dried mint

Middle Eastern food is known to be rich in vegetables; we consume them quite abundantly both in raw and cooked forms. When I was growing up, there wasn't a single dinner we had without a bowl of this freshly chopped salata as a regular accompaniment to every dish. My sisters and I used to love it simply scooped on top of my mom's Roz Bi Shaariya (page 67). The dressing and the mix of vegetables varies from family to family; you can even make it with just cucumbers and tomatoes if that's all you have on hand, along with a simple squeeze of lemon juice and a drizzle of pomegranate molasses. This dressing, however, is my go-to. I often prepare it in a large jar and keep it in the fridge to use throughout the week.

1 TO MAKE THE SALATA: In a medium salad bowl, combine the cucumbers, tomato, onion, bell pepper, and parsley. Sprinkle with the ¼ teaspoon salt.

2 TO MAKE THE DRESSING: Add the oil, lemon juice, pomegranate molasses, sumac, mint, and ½ teaspoon salt to a jar or container with a lid. Seal the jar or container and shake well until combined.

3 Drizzle ¼ cup (60 ml) of the dressing over the salad. Toss to combine well. Taste and adjust for more dressing as desired. Seal the jar or container, refrigerate, and use as needed.

4 Garnish with dried mint, then serve immediately, or let chill in the refrigerator for no more than 1 hour.

Note

This salata is perfect to pair with any rice or meat dish. It can also be used in sandwiches with Shawarma (page 88), Shish Tawook (page 91), and Iraqi Aroog (page145).

Dill Potato Salad

YIELD: 6 to 8 servings

PREP TIME: 10 minutes, plus 2 hours chilling

COOK TIME: 15 minutes

◇◇◇◇◇

POTATO SALAD

2 teaspoons kosher salt

5 medium yellow potatoes (about 3 pounds, or 1.3 kg), peeled and cut into 1- to 1½-inch (2.5 to 4 cm) chunks

1 large bunch fresh dill, finely chopped and thick stems removed

6 green onions, finely chopped

1½ cups (75 g) finely chopped fresh parsley

2 cups (280 g) finely chopped pickled turnips (or substitute with 3 large dill pickles, finely chopped)

DRESSING

1 cup (240 ml) plain, whole-milk yogurt

½ cup (120 ml) mayonnaise

½ cup (120 g) sweet relish

2 tablespoons Dijon mustard

1½ teaspoons ground Aleppo pepper (or substitute with 1 teaspoon paprika plus ¼ teaspoon cayenne pepper)

1 teaspoon kosher salt

This is not your average mayo-heavy potato salad; it's jazzed up with plenty of fresh herbs and has a dressing that relies on a base of yogurt for tartness and lightness. Although not a salad that's native to the Middle Eastern region, potato salads have quickly become favorites in many Arab households, especially those of us living in diaspora. We don't say no to carbs in the form of potatoes. To add a Middle Eastern touch, I make this with lots of dill, parsley, and green onion. The dressing is a quick mix of yogurt, relish, mustard, a little bit of mayo, and Aleppo pepper. If you can find pink pickled turnips, use them to brighten up the salad and add some color. Make sure you chill this in the fridge for at least two hours before you serve it.

1 **TO MAKE THE POTATO SALAD:** Fill a large pot more than halfway with water and place over medium heat. Add the 2 teaspoons salt and bring to a boil.

2 Add the potatoes to the boiling water and boil until fork-tender, 10 to 12 minutes. Drain in a colander and let cool completely.

3 **MEANWHILE, MAKE THE DRESSING:** In a small bowl, whisk together the yogurt, mayonnaise, relish, Dijon mustard, Aleppo pepper, and 1 teaspoon salt.

4 Place the cooled potatoes, dill, green onions, parsley and pickles in a large bowl and add the dressing. Toss to combine well.

5 Refrigerate for at least 2 hours before serving for best results.

Tahini Cabbage Slaw

YIELD: 6 servings

PREP TIME: 20 minutes

◇◇◇◇◇

CABBAGE SLAW

14 ounces (400 g) white or purple
    cabbage, shredded

7 ounces (200 g) carrots, shredded

3 green onions, finely chopped

¼ cup (13 g) finely chopped fresh
    parsley

1 cup (145 g) raisins

½ teaspoon kosher salt

DRESSING

½ cup (120 ml) plain, whole-milk
    yogurt

½ cup (120 ml) tahini

¼ cup (60 ml) fresh lemon juice
    (about 2 lemons), plus more
    if needed

2 teaspoons honey

1 teaspoon kosher salt, plus more
    if needed

¼ teaspoon black pepper

1 large clove garlic

1 large green onion, roughly chopped

¼ cup (13 g) roughly chopped fresh
    parsley

I love shredded cabbage salads, but I shied away from them for so long, simply because I found hand-slicing a head of cabbage too tedious. But once I started to use a mandoline, which changed my life, my cabbage intake saw a huge spike. Nowadays, you can even find ready-shredded cabbage at most grocery stores, which would make this salad a breeze to make. I make this often to serve alongside grilled chicken or steak as a welcome change from our normal chopped salad, Salata (page 44). The green yogurt and tahini dressing alone is worth making—you'll want to drizzle it on everything.

1 TO MAKE THE CABBAGE SLAW: In a medium salad bowl, combine the cabbage and carrots. Add the green onion, parsley, and raisins. Sprinkle with the ½ teaspoon salt.

2 TO MAKE THE DRESSING: Place the yogurt, tahini, lemon juice, honey, salt, pepper, garlic, green onion, and parsley in a small blender and process until smooth. You may need to add a few tablespoons of water to loosen the dressing to help it blend well. Taste and adjust for more salt and/or lemon juice if needed.

3 Drizzle the dressing over the salad. Toss to combine well and serve.

Bulgur Salad

YIELD: 4 servings

PREP TIME: 10 minutes, plus 2 hours chilling

COOK TIME: 25 minutes

◇◇◇◇◇

BULGUR

2 tablespoons olive oil

½ small yellow onion, finely chopped

½ teaspoon kosher salt

1 cup (180 g) coarse bulgur (see Note), rinsed and drained

SALAD

3 small Persian cucumbers, small diced

1 large tomato, small diced

1 large red bell pepper, small diced

½ cup (25 g) finely chopped fresh parsley

3 green onions, finely chopped

¼ cup (35 g) raisins

¼ cup (30 g) slivered almonds (or substitute with other nuts or seeds)

DRESSING

¼ cup (60 ml) fresh lemon juice

2 tablespoons pomegranate molasses

2 tablespoons olive oil

½ teaspoon kosher salt

¼ teaspoon black pepper

Bulgur is a common grain in Iraq and across the Middle East, often cooked into a pilaf as a replacement for rice. I absolutely love the nutty flavor of bulgur and believe that it is underrated in the Western world. It's also a healthy grain: it's more nutritious than rice and has a higher fiber content than even brown rice. Since it is what I call a "sturdy" grain (it's hard to mess up and holds up quite well to moisture), it is perfect to use in salads. I make this salad on a regular rotation; my husband and I enjoy it as part of our meal-prepped lunches. The almonds and raisins are absolute musts. Make sure you let it chill in the fridge for a few hours if you can, so it'll be extra delicious.

1 TO MAKE THE BULGUR: In a medium saucepan, heat the oil over medium heat. Add the onion and cook, stirring often, until softened, 5 to 6 minutes.

2 Add the salt, bulgur, and 1½ cups (360 ml) of water. Bring to a boil, then cover and let simmer over low heat for 20 minutes. Fluff it with a fork and check doneness; the grains should be soft but not mushy. If the grains are not soft, add 2 tablespoons of water, cover again, and let stand for 10 more minutes with the heat off.

3 TO MAKE THE SALAD: Transfer the cooked bulgur to a medium bowl. Add the cucumbers, tomato, red pepper, parsley, green onions, and raisins.

4 TO MAKE THE DRESSING: Add the lemon juice, pomegranate molasses, oil, salt, and pepper to a small jar or bowl. Whisk or seal the jar and shake the ingredients to incorporate well.

5 Pour the dressing over the salad and toss to combine well. Refrigerate for at least 2 hours.

6 Toast the slivered almonds in a small, dry skillet over medium heat for 3 to 4 minutes, until lightly golden, stirring continuously. Add them to the salad right before serving.

Note

If you can't find coarse bulgur, you can use fine bulgur, but it requires no cooking. Simply soak 1 cup (180 g) of fine bulgur in 2 cups (480 ml) of boiling water for 10 to 12 minutes. Season with ½ teaspoon kosher salt, drizzle with 2 tablespoons of olive oil, and then fluff it with a fork.

Arugula & Pomegranate Salad

YIELD: 2 servings

PREP TIME: 10 minutes

◇◇◇◇◇

3½ cups (70 g) arugula

2 tablespoons olive oil

¼ cup (10 g) fresh mint leaves

⅓ cup (70 g) pomegranate arils

¼ cup (30 g) shredded Parmesan cheese

¼ cup (40 g) chopped pistachios

1 tablespoon pomegranate molasses

Kosher salt and black pepper

This salad is what I often throw together when I want a "no chopping" salad that I can make in just a few minutes. I first had it at an upscale restaurant in Kuwait, and I was pleasantly surprised by the combination of pomegranate and Parmesan cheese. The tartness and saltiness work so well together alongside the pepperiness of the arugula. Garnishing it with chopped pistachios adds texture and elevates it, but feel free to use any other seeds or nuts you have on hand.

1 In a large bowl, massage the arugula with the oil.

2 Add the mint leaves, pomegranate arils, Parmesan, and pistachios to the bowl. Drizzle with the pomegranate molasses and season with salt and pepper.

3 Toss to combine well and serve.

Za'atar & Feta Pasta Salad

YIELD: 4 servings

PREP TIME: 10 minutes, plus 1 hour chilling

COOK TIME: 10 minutes

◇◇◇◇◇

PASTA SALAD

8 ounces (225 g) pasta of choice (such as cavatelli, farfalle, or fusilli)

2 small Persian cucumbers, finely chopped

½ cup (55 g) sliced black olives

½ cup (30 g) finely chopped green onions

½ cup (25 g) finely chopped fresh parsley

½ cup (60 g) chopped sun-dried tomatoes

⅔ cup (100 g) crumbled feta cheese

DRESSING

¼ cup (60 ml) fresh lemon juice

2 tablespoons za'atar

¼ cup (60 ml) olive oil

½ teaspoon kosher salt

2 tablespoons Dijon mustard

2 tablespoons honey

Pasta salads are not traditional to Middle Eastern cuisine, but like potato salad, my mom made them quite often when I was growing up. Her version would have chicken and a lot of mayonnaise, which I loved. But this version is the one I make the most often. The dressing has a base of olive oil and lemon juice combined with herby za'atar, Dijon mustard, and honey. You can use any pasta shape you like, but smaller ones work best, as they'll be the same size as the other ingredients. I load it up with black olives, sun-dried tomatoes, herbs, and the most important component: salty feta cheese. This salad tastes even better after being refrigerated for a few hours.

1 TO MAKE THE PASTA SALAD: Cook the pasta to al dente according to the package directions.

2 Meanwhile, add the cucumbers, olives, green onions, parsley, sun-dried tomatoes, and feta to a medium salad bowl.

3 When the pasta is cooked, drain and run under cold water to cool it, then add it to the salad bowl.

4 TO MAKE THE DRESSING: In a small bowl, whisk together the lemon juice, za'atar, oil, salt, Dijon mustard, and honey until well combined.

5 Pour the dressing over the salad and toss to combine well.

6 Refrigerate for at least 1 hour before serving.

Lemony Bean Salad

YIELD: 4 servings

PREP TIME: 10 minutes, plus 30 minutes chilling

◇◇◇◇◇

BEAN SALAD

38 ounces (1.1 kg) mixed canned
    beans, drained and rinsed

1 cup (50 g) finely chopped parsley

2 Roma tomatoes, small diced

½ large red onion, small diced

DRESSING

⅓ cup (80 ml) fresh lemon juice, plus
    more if needed

½ cup (120 ml) olive oil

1½ teaspoons kosher salt, plus more
    if needed

⅛ teaspoon black pepper

This bean salad is a quick, filling, and nutritious lunch fix that I make quite regularly. Beans are a blank canvas for absorbing bright flavors. That's why this lemony olive oil dressing works so well. I love using a medley of beans like red and white kidney beans, chickpeas, and black-eyed peas. Also, do not skip the onions; they are a necessary component. You can prepare the salad in advance, as it keeps quite well in the fridge and tastes even better the next day.

1 TO MAKE THE BEAN SALAD: Place the beans in a medium salad bowl. Add the parsley, tomatoes, and onion.

2 TO MAKE THE DRESSING: In a small bowl, whisk together the lemon juice, oil, salt, and pepper.

3 Pour the dressing over the salad and toss to combine well. Taste and adjust for more salt and/or lemon juice if needed.

4 Refrigerate for at least 30 minutes before serving.

Crumbled Falafel Salad

YIELD: 4 to 6 servings

PREP TIME: 15 minutes, plus overnight soaking

COOK TIME: 35 minutes

◇◇◇◇◇

FALAFEL

2½ cups (500 g) dried chickpeas

6 cups (1.4 L) cold water

½ teaspoon baking soda

2 small yellow onions, cut into quarters

10 large cloves garlic

2 cups (100 g) packed roughly chopped fresh parsley

1 cup (40 g) packed roughly chopped fresh cilantro

1 teaspoon baking powder

¾ cup (180 ml) plus 3 tablespoons olive oil, divided

2 teaspoons kosher salt

3 teaspoons ground cumin

3 teaspoons ground coriander

½ teaspoon black pepper

DRESSING

½ cup (120 ml) tahini

¼ cup (60 ml) fresh lemon juice

1 large clove garlic

1 green onion, roughly chopped

6 leaves basil

¼ cup (13 g) packed roughly chopped fresh parsley

½ teaspoon kosher salt

Falafel need no introduction. They have quickly gained popularity across the world for their distinctive taste and versatility. Falafel is considered a street food in Middle Eastern countries, often served in a wrap with tahini sauce and fresh vegetables. The idea for this crumbled falafel salad came to me when I was thinking about how street vendors squash the falafel into the bread when they assemble the wrap, breaking it up so that it's easier to roll. So, why not make crumbled falafel as a "crouton" topping to salads? It also completely skips the shaping and deep-frying steps, which turns this into an easy and quick lunch. I found that spreading the falafel mixture in a sheet pan and baking it in intervals, flipping it in sections in between, results in a similar texture to "squashed falafel." You'll get lots of crispy bits and some soft fluffy bits and be snacking right from the pan. Please note that when making this recipe, always use dried chickpeas, never canned, as the latter have too much moisture to form a firm dough.

1 TO MAKE THE FALAFEL: Place the dried chickpeas in a large bowl and cover them with the cold water. Stir in the baking soda and leave them to soak overnight; they will double in size. When ready to use, drain the chickpeas and pat them dry.

2 Preheat the oven to 450°F (230°C) and place a rack on the bottom.

3 Add the yellow onions and 10 garlic cloves to a large food processor and pulse for a few seconds until finely chopped. Add the soaked chickpeas, 2 cups (100 g) parsley, cilantro, baking powder, 3 tablespoons of the oil, 2 teaspoons salt, cumin, coriander, and pepper. Process for 5 to 7 minutes, until the ingredients are mashed together and the mixture has a dough-like consistency, pausing to scrape the bottom of the food processor and ensure all the ingredients are incorporated. If the mixture is still crumbly, continue to pulse in the food processor until it holds together.

4 Pour ½ cup (120 ml) of the oil into a rimmed half sheet pan (18 x 13 inches, or 46 x 33 cm) lined with parchment paper and spread it evenly. Place the falafel mixture into the pan and flatten it using your hands, covering the surface of the sheet pan in an even layer. Do not pack it down too much.

CONTINUED ▶

SALAD

1 to 2 hearts romaine lettuce, roughly chopped

6 small Persian cucumbers, finely chopped

¼ medium red onion, finely chopped

¼ cup (36 g) chopped pickled turnips (or dill pickles)

1 large tomato, chopped (optional)

5 Bake on the bottom rack for 20 minutes, or until the edges start to turn slightly golden. Remove the pan from the oven and, using a spatula, break up and flip pieces of the falafel over, working your way across the entire sheet pan. The aim is to flip it over in sections; it is fine if some of the falafel pieces break up or crumble, since the result will be a combination of larger crispy chunks and smaller crumbles. Drizzle the falafel with the remaining ¼ cup (60 ml) oil and bake for another 15 minutes, or until golden brown. Remove from the oven and test a few pieces; there should be a mixture of dark, crunchy pieces and softer pieces. If you want more crunch and color, return it to the oven for a few more minutes on the broil setting.

6 WHILE THE FALAFEL BAKES, MAKE THE DRESSING: Add the tahini, lemon juice, garlic clove, green onion, basil, ¼ cup (13 g) parsley, ½ teaspoon salt, and ¼ cup (60 ml) of water to a blender and process until a smooth and runny dressing forms. You may need to add a bit more water to loosen the dressing.

7 TO MAKE THE SALAD: In a large salad bowl, combine the lettuce, cucumbers, red onion, pickled turnips, and tomato (if using). Add most of the dressing and toss to combine well. Top with the falafel croutons, drizzle with the remaining salad dressing, and then serve.

Notes

+ Store any falafel leftovers in an airtight container, then drizzle with olive oil and heat in an oven or air fryer to crisp up again before using. The uncooked falafel dough can also be refrigerated in an airtight container for 2 to 3 days until ready to cook.

+ You can also use this falafel recipe to make classic deep-fried falafel. Shape 2 tablespoons of the falafel mixture into balls or discs. Heat about 3 inches (7.5 cm) of vegetable oil in a deep skillet to 350 to 375°F (175 to 190°C). Deep-fry the balls for 3 to 4 minutes, until golden, then transfer to paper towels to absorb excess oil. Serve immediately with the salad dressing or Tarator (page 30).

Iraqi Timman Ahmar
RED RICE

YIELD: 6 servings
PREP TIME: 10 minutes
COOK TIME: 30 minutes

◇◇◇◇◇

2 dried limes

¼ cup (60 ml) vegetable oil

1 medium yellow onion, finely chopped

1½ teaspoons kosher salt, divided

⅓ cup (70 g) tomato paste

3 cups (720 ml) chicken broth (see Notes)

2 cups (400 g) long-grain white basmati rice, rinsed until the water runs clear and drained completely

Note

To serve this red rice with chicken, make homemade chicken broth by boiling 3 or 4 bone-in chicken legs in 8 cups (2 L) of water, along with 1 quartered onion, 1 large carrot cut in half, 1½ teaspoons of kosher salt, 3 bay leaves, and 6 cardamom pods. Boil for 45 minutes, or until the chicken is cooked. Remove the chicken from the broth and lay it on a sheet pan. Brush the tops of the legs with 1 tablespoon of tomato paste mixed with 1 tablespoon of olive oil. Broil for 5 minutes, or until browned. Use the strained broth to cook the rice, then serve the chicken legs over the rice with Salata (page 44).

Iraqis are known for their wide variety of rice dishes. The word *timman* translates to "rice," but only in the Iraqi dialect. The real Arabic word for "rice" is *roz*. So, you may be wondering why it is known as "timman" throughout the country. Legend has it that during the British occupation in the 1920s and '30s, the British brought with them an Indian brand of rice called Ten Men. Iraqis would often hear rice being referred to as "ten men," which led to the modern-day word *timman*. I'm not sure if this story is true, but I do love the sound of it. Red rice is one of many rice-based side dishes you'll find served in Iraqi homes. It's typically made with fresh chicken stock, tomato paste, and dried lime for an earthy and tart flavor. The chicken used to make the stock is also sometimes broiled and served on top of the rice, taking this from a side dish to a main (see Note), especially when served with Salata (page 44).

1 Bring a kettle or pot of water to a boil. Place the dried limes in a small bowl, pour the hot water on top, and let sit for 5 minutes, or until softened. Once they are soft, remove the limes from the bowl and use a knife to make 2 or 3 slits in each one to allow the flavor to be extracted.

2 In a large pot, heat the oil over medium heat. Add the onion, sprinkle with ½ teaspoon of the salt, and cook, stirring often, until softened and translucent, 4 to 5 minutes.

3 Add the tomato paste and dried limes and cook for 1 to 2 minutes to caramelize the tomato paste.

4 Add the broth and remaining 1 teaspoon salt to the pot and stir. Bring the pot to a rolling boil. Taste and adjust the broth for salt (it should taste noticeably salty; you may need to add more salt depending on the broth you are using).

5 Add the rice. Wait for it to come back to a rolling boil, then let boil for 2 to 3 minutes. Cover with a tight-fitting lid, reduce the heat to low, and let cook for 20 minutes, undisturbed.

6 Remove from the heat and gently fluff the rice with a fork or wooden spoon. Cover again and let stand for another 10 minutes before serving.

SEE RECIPE PHOTO ON OVERLEAF ▶

Turkish Bulgur Pilaf

YIELD: 6 servings
PREP TIME: 5 minutes
COOK TIME: 40 minutes

◇◇◇◇◇

1 tablespoon unsalted butter

2 tablespoons olive oil

1 large onion, finely chopped

1 large red bell pepper, finely chopped

4 large cloves garlic, minced

1½ teaspoons kosher salt

¼ teaspoon black pepper

1 tablespoon tomato paste

1 tablespoon sweet red pepper paste

1 teaspoon dried mint

2 cups (360 g) coarse bulgur, rinsed and drained

4 cups (960 ml) chicken broth

FOR GARNISHING AND SERVING

Fresh mint leaves (optional)

Plain, whole-milk yogurt

Dried mint

Bulgur is a type of cracked wheat that is parboiled, dried, and then ground into various sizes. Fine bulgur is used in salads like tabouli and requires no cooking; it is simply soaked in liquid. Medium and coarse bulgur are used to make dishes like this bulgur pilaf. Its cooking process is similar to that of rice, using a bulgur-to-liquid ratio of 1:2. When I was growing up, my mom cooked bulgur regularly instead of rice, often making "red bulgur" using tomato paste and adding chickpeas, and sometimes making "yellow bulgur" with onions and mushrooms (see One-Pot Chicken & Mushroom Bulgur on page 134). This Turkish-style bulgur pilaf is one we grew accustomed to, as we frequented Turkish restaurants and always enjoyed it alongside grilled meat. The distinguishing features of Turkish pilaf are the use of red pepper paste along with tomato paste and the addition of dried mint, which gives it a unique and delicious flavor. This dish is very quick to make and versatile as a side to many meals.

1 In a large saucepan or skillet, melt the butter along with the oil over medium heat.

2 Add the onion and cook, stirring often, until softened, 4 to 5 minutes. Add the bell pepper and cook for 2 to 3 minutes, until softened. Add the garlic and cook for 1 minute. Season with the salt and pepper, stir, and cook for 1 to 2 more minutes.

3 Add the tomato and red pepper pastes, cooking and stirring until combined, for 1 minute.

4 Add the dried mint, followed by the bulgur, mixing until well combined. Add the broth and bring to a boil for 3 minutes. Reduce the heat to low, cover with the lid, and let simmer for 25 minutes.

5 Fluff up the bulgur, garnish with mint leaves (if using) and serve with yogurt sprinkled with dried mint.

Roz Bi Shaariya
VERMICELLI RICE

YIELD: 6 servings
PREP TIME: 10 minutes
COOK TIME: 30 minutes

◇◇◇◇◇

3 tablespoons vegetable oil

½ cup (50 g) vermicelli noodles (see Note)

3½ cups (840 ml) boiling chicken broth or water

1½ teaspoons kosher salt

2 cups (400 g) long-grain white basmati rice, rinsed until the water runs clear and drained completely

FOR GARNISHING (OPTIONAL)

¼ cup pine nuts (35 g) or slivered almonds (30 g)

Handful finely chopped fresh parsley

When there are no guests over or special occasions, everyday Middle Eastern home cooking is usually rice with some sort of vegetable and meat stew (more on those in the Soups & Stews section on page 192). The most popular type of rice served is long-grain basmati rice, dotted with short golden vermicelli noodles. Not to be confused with the Asian thin rice noodles, the vermicelli used in this rice pilaf is wheat-based. The vermicelli is first toasted in oil or butter until golden brown, then the rice, broth, and seasoning are added. This fluffy rice is quite addictive and delicious even on its own with a side of Salata (page 44).

1 In a large pot, heat the oil over medium heat. Add the noodles and cook for 1 to 2 minutes, stirring continuously, until they turn golden brown.

2 Add the boiling broth or water and salt to the pot. (If using broth, taste the liquid after you add it to the pot and before adding the salt. Add as much salt as needed to ensure the broth tastes noticeably salty; alternatively, some broths have a high salt content, so you may need less salt.) Bring to a rolling boil, then add the rice. Wait for it to come back to a rolling boil, then reduce the heat to low and cover with a tight-fitting lid. Let cook for 20 minutes, undisturbed.

3 Remove the lid and gently fluff the rice with a fork or wooden spoon. Cover again and let stand for another 10 minutes before serving.

4 If garnishing with the pine nuts or almonds, in a small dry skillet, toast the nuts for 2 to 3 minutes over medium heat, until golden, stirring continuously.

5 Serve the rice on a platter, topped with the toasted pine nuts or almonds (if using) and chopped parsley (if using).

Note

You can make this recipe with only white basmati rice and no vermicelli noodles. Simply omit the noodles and use a rice-to-water ratio of 1:1.5 for long-grain white basmati rice.

Iraqi Timman Bagilla
FAVA BEAN AND DILL RICE

YIELD: 6 servings
PREP TIME: 10 minutes
COOK TIME: 35 minutes

◇◇◇◇◇

3 cups (600 g) long-grain white basmati rice, rinsed until the water runs clear and drained completely

7 tablespoons olive oil, divided

1 large onion, finely chopped

28 ounces (800 g) frozen cooked and peeled fava beans (or substitute cooked or canned lima beans)

3 cups (150 g) packed finely chopped fresh dill, thick stems removed

2½ teaspoons kosher salt

½ teaspoon black pepper

4 cups (960 ml) chicken or vegetable broth, divided

This is one of the most quintessential Iraqi rice dishes. Beloved across the country, timman bagilla uses vibrant green fava beans and lots of fresh dill and is enjoyed mainly in the spring and summer, when fresh beans are abundant in the markets. I make this at least once every few weeks for my husband, as it is a dear favorite in our household. It creates a light and balanced meal, with protein from the beans, especially when served alongside a bowl of plain yogurt and Salata (page 44). It is mostly vegetarian, but sometimes bone-in chicken legs are crisped up and served on top of the rice. This rice dish is also common in Iran and known there as *baghali polo*.

1 Place the rinsed rice in a bowl, cover with water, and let soak for 10 minutes.

2 In a medium pot, heat 5 tablespoons of the oil over medium heat. Add the onion and cook, stirring often, until softened and translucent, 5 to 7 minutes.

3 Add the fava beans and let them thaw in the pot for 5 minutes. (Or add the lima beans, if using instead, and warm them through for 5 minutes.) Add the dill, salt, pepper, and 2 cups (480 ml) of the broth to the pot. Cover with the lid and cook for 5 minutes.

4 Add the remaining 2 cups (480 ml) broth to the pot and bring to a boil over high heat. Taste and adjust the liquid for more salt if needed; it should taste noticeably salty.

5 Add the rice to the pot along with the remaining 2 tablespoons oil and bring to a boil again for 2 to 3 minutes. The liquid level should be about even with the surface of the rice (not much more). Cover the pot, reduce the heat to low, and let cook for 20 minutes, undisturbed.

6 Fluff the rice with a fork or wooden spoon and check on it. If it is still slightly undercooked, add ¼ cup (60 ml) of water, cover it again, and let cook for 10 more minutes before serving.

Roz Asfar
FRAGRANT YELLOW RICE

YIELD: 6 servings
PREP TIME: 10 minutes
COOK TIME: 30 minutes

◇◇◇◇◇

¼ cup (60 ml) olive oil

1 small yellow onion, finely chopped

½ teaspoon whole peppercorns

5 whole cloves

5 whole green cardamom pods

2 cinnamon sticks

2 teaspoons kosher salt, or more to taste

1 teaspoon ground turmeric

3 cups (550 g) long-grain white basmati rice, rinsed until the water runs clear and drained completely

4½ cups (1 L) chicken broth

Fragrant yellow rice is commonplace at Middle Eastern restaurants, often served as a side in shawarma platters. It gets its vibrant yellow color from the addition of turmeric or, in other variations, saffron. I love using an abundance of fragrant whole spices in the broth, which lend it a delicious flavor and inviting aroma. If you want to make it extra fancy for guests, toast some almonds and raisins and sprinkle them on top. Serve as a side to main dishes, such as Sheet-Pan Chicken Shawarma (page 88).

1 In a large pot, heat the oil for 1 minute over medium heat. Add the onion and cook, stirring often, until softened and translucent, 5 to 6 minutes.

2 Add the peppercorns, cloves, cardamom, and cinnamon sticks to the pot and cook, stirring continuously, for a few more minutes until the spices are toasted and fragrant. Add the salt and turmeric and stir to combine with the onion and spices.

3 Add the rice and stir it gently to combine with the onion and spices. Add the broth and bring to a rolling boil over medium heat, then cover the pot with a tight-fitting lid, reduce the heat to low, and let cook for 20 minutes, undisturbed.

4 Turn off the heat, remove the lid, and gently fluff the rice with a fork or wooden spoon. Cover again and let rest for 10 minutes. Before serving, pick out and discard the peppercorns, cloves, cardamom pods and cinnamon sticks (see Note).

Note

If you want to avoid picking out the whole spices from the cooked rice, you can toast them in a dry skillet for a few minutes, or until fragrant, then place them in a cheesecloth and wrap it with kitchen twine or place them in a small mesh tea ball.

Pan-Fried Curried Cauliflower Fritters

YIELD: 15 to 20 pieces

PREP TIME: 15 minutes

COOK TIME: 15 minutes

◇◇◇◇◇

CAULIFLOWER FRITTERS

½ large head cauliflower, cut into florets

½ large yellow potato, peeled and grated

½ cup (25 g) chopped fresh parsley

½ cup (30 g) chopped green onions

2 eggs, beaten

3 teaspoons curry powder

1 teaspoon ground coriander

2 teaspoons kosher salt

½ teaspoon black pepper

¼ cup (30 g) all-purpose flour

¼ cup (60 ml) olive oil, plus more if needed

MINT YOGURT SAUCE (OPTIONAL)

½ cup (120 ml) plain, whole-milk yogurt

1 tablespoon mayonnaise

1 teaspoon dried mint

⅛ teaspoon black pepper

¼ teaspoon kosher salt

My mom used to always make fried cauliflower for us to stuff into fresh Iraqi *samoon* (buns), with sliced tomatoes, parsley, and onions. Keeping the cauliflower florets intact, she would steam them to soften them and then dip them in an egg mixture seasoned with curry powder. She would then shallow-fry them in oil and serve them warm and golden brown. I still make them her way to this day. But I wanted to adapt her classic recipe to a flatter fritter shape that's made more substantial by the addition of grated potatoes and fragrant herbs. This version of cauliflower fritters is a favorite with my kids, especially when served with a quick mint yogurt sauce for dipping or smearing onto sandwiches.

1 TO MAKE THE CAULIFLOWER FRITTERS: Place 1 or 2 inches (2.5 to 5 cm) of water in a small pot and place a steamer basket inside; bring the water to a boil. Place the cauliflower florets in the steamer basket, cover, and cook until tender, 4 to 8 minutes depending on the size of the florets. (You can also steam the cauliflower in a microwave using a microwave steamer basket.)

2 Transfer the steamed cauliflower to a large bowl. Lightly mash it using a potato masher until the florets are broken down but not overly mushy.

3 Add the potato, parsley, green onions, beaten eggs, curry powder, coriander, 2 teaspoons salt, ½ teaspoon pepper, and flour. Mix well using a spoon or your hands until all the ingredients are combined.

4 In a large skillet, heat the oil over medium heat. Place a heaping spoonful of fritter batter into the hot oil and gently flatten it into a rough circular shape. Continue spooning the fritters in to cover the surface of the skillet without overcrowding. Shallow-fry each side for 1 to 2 minutes, until golden and crispy. Transfer to a paper towel–lined plate to absorb excess oil. (You may need to add more oil until all the fritter batter is cooked.)

5 TO MAKE THE MINT YOGURT SAUCE (OPTIONAL): In a small bowl, whisk together the yogurt, mayonnaise, mint, ⅛ teaspoon pepper, and ¼ teaspoon salt until combined.

6 Serve the fritters with the sauce (if using) for dipping or into sandwiches.

Turkish Cheese Börek
PHYLLO CHEESE PIE

YIELD: 6 servings

PREP TIME: 20 minutes, plus 2 hours thawing

COOK TIME: 25 minutes

◇◇◇◇◇

PHYLLO PASTRY

1 package (1 pound, or 454 g) frozen phyllo dough (16 to 20 sheets)

¼ teaspoon nigella seeds

1 teaspoon white sesame seeds

CHEESE FILLING

4½ ounces (130 g) crumbled feta cheese

1⅔ cups (185 g) shredded mozzarella cheese

¼ cup (25 g) grated Parmesan cheese (or use more feta)

½ cup (25 g) finely chopped fresh parsley

¼ cup (40 g) finely chopped white onion (or substitute green onions)

1 teaspoon nigella seeds

EGG WASH

3 tablespoons unsalted butter, melted

½ cup (120 ml) olive oil

1 large egg

¼ cup (60 ml) whole milk

Börek is a popular Turkish side dish that features thin dough, usually thin yufka or phyllo pastry, layered with butter and stuffed with various fillings: cheese, meat, or vegetables. It is surprisingly easy to make using store-bought phyllo dough and the delicious cheese mixture found in this recipe. This pie will look impressive on your table when it bakes to golden perfection, its surface dotted with sesame and nigella seeds. This is quite possibly my favorite pie of all time; I can never just have one piece. The combination of herbs, the three types of cheese, and the chopped white onion in the filling make it irresistible! When making it, it's important to make sure you cut it into pieces before you bake it.

1 TO PREPARE THE PHYLLO PASTRY: Bring the phyllo dough to room temperature by thawing on the counter for 2 hours or in the refrigerator overnight.

2 Preheat the oven to 350°F (175°C) on the convection setting (if you do not have this setting, use the bake setting) and place an oven rack in the middle.

3 TO MAKE THE CHEESE FILLING: In a medium bowl, mix together the feta, mozzarella, and Parmesan cheeses. Add the parsley, onion, and 1 teaspoon nigella seeds and mix well to combine.

4 TO MAKE THE EGG WASH: In a small bowl, whisk together the melted butter, oil, egg, and milk until combined.

5 Open the phyllo dough package and lay the pastry sheets on a flat surface, loosely covered with a kitchen towel.

6 Cut a piece of parchment paper that fits the dimensions of a 10 x 12-inch (25 x 30 cm) baking dish and place it inside the dish. Use a pastry brush to brush the bottom and sides of the dish with egg wash, right over the parchment paper. Place 2 to 4 phyllo sheets on the base of the dish, allowing the pastry to overhang all sides, so there are at least 2 inches (5 cm) of excess dough. Place the sheets slightly offset from each other so that there is enough dough overhanging; this excess overhang will be folded over the topmost layer at the end to ensure the filling stays securely inside and does not ooze out. Brush these sheets with egg wash until well saturated.

CONTINUED ▶

7 Set aside 2 phyllo sheets to use for the top of the börek. Divide the remaining sheets in half. Use half of the sheets for the next few steps to layer the börek. Pick up one sheet at a time, tear it into 2 or 3 pieces, and scrunch up the pieces with your hands to create crumpled-up dough (like you would crumple up a piece of paper). Place the crumpled-up dough pieces loosely in the dish, spreading them out evenly across the surface area; crumpling the pastry will create air pockets for a softer, lighter börek.

8 Use the pastry brush to gently brush egg wash all over the crumpled phyllo sheets, then spoon all the cheese mixture into the baking dish, on top of the crumpled-up dough, creating an even layer.

9 Repeat the same tearing, scrunching, and crumpling of the dough with the remaining half of the phyllo sheets, then place them over the cheese mixture in an even layer and brush them with egg wash.

10 Fold the overhanging phyllo dough over the topmost layer and pat down gently to flatten. Place the reserved 2 sheets on top in a smooth, flat layer; this layer should cover the full surface of the börek. If you must trim some excess dough to create an even layer, do so. Brush the top with the remaining egg wash.

11 Using a sharp knife, gently cut the börek into 12 equal-size squares, using a sawing motion to avoid disturbing the phyllo dough too much and to keep the pieces intact. Sprinkle the surface with the ¼ teaspoon nigella seeds and the sesame seeds.

12 Place in the oven on the middle rack and bake for 25 to 30 minutes, until the top is golden brown and the filling is heated through and melted. You may broil the top for a few minutes, if required, to achieve a golden color. Let cool for 10 minutes. Use a sharp knife to gently slice into the precut squares and serve.

Notes

+ You can use a different-size baking dish by simply cutting the phyllo dough to fit. The thickness of the börek may differ depending on the size of the pan; therefore, adjust the bake time as needed.

+ You can layer the pie ahead of time and keep it in the fridge, ready to bake closer to serving time. Leftover pieces can be easily frozen and reheated in the oven.

Lahm Bi Ajeen
SPICED GROUND BEEF FLATBREAD

YIELD: 6 servings

PREP TIME: 20 minutes, plus 1 hour resting

COOK TIME: 30 minutes

◇◇◇◇◇

DOUGH

2 teaspoons instant yeast

1 tablespoon granulated sugar

1 cup (240 ml) lukewarm water

2½ cups (300 g) all-purpose flour, plus more for dusting

1 teaspoon kosher salt

¼ cup (60 ml) olive oil, plus more for greasing

FILLING

1 large onion, finely chopped

½ bunch fresh parsley, finely chopped

1 pound (454 g) lean ground beef

3½ ounces (100 g) tomato paste

3½ ounces (100 ml) tomato passata (puree)

1 tablespoon pomegranate molasses

1 teaspoon black pepper

1 teaspoon kosher salt

½ teaspoon curry powder

1 teaspoon ground allspice

¼ teaspoon ground cinnamon

FOR GARNISHING AND SERVING

8 to 10 lemon wedges

½ medium red onion, sliced

1 tablespoon sumac

½ cup (25 g) roughly chopped fresh parsley

This is one of my favorite recipes from my mom. This ground beef flatbread is common across many Middle Eastern countries, most notably in Turkey as *lahmacun*, in Iraq as *lahm bi ajeen*, and in Levantine countries as *meat manakish*. It's made using ground lamb, beef, or a mix of the two, as well as onion, parsley, tomato paste, and pomegranate molasses. The distinguishing feature in my mom's recipe is her ample use of warm spices that really take it to another level. She would serve it as a light dinner with a steaming cup of hot tea; it can also be served as an appetizer. We even turn leftovers into a breakfast treat by cracking an egg in the middle of a baked lahm bi ajeen and broiling it in the oven until the egg is set. If you're intimidated by making dough from scratch, feel free to use ready-made pizza dough, or skip the dough altogether and use thin tortillas for a wonderful alternative, making for a weeknight-friendly version (see Note on page 79).

1 TO MAKE THE DOUGH: Place the yeast and sugar in a small bowl with the lukewarm water and mix with a spoon. Let stand for 2 to 3 minutes.

2 Using a stand mixer with a dough hook, place the flour and salt in the mixing bowl and start mixing on low speed. Add the oil to the bowl and continue to mix until the oil is fully incorporated into the flour. Gradually add the water-yeast mixture and continue to mix on medium speed. Once the water is fully incorporated, the dough will start to form. Continue kneading for at least 5 to 7 minutes. The dough is ready when it feels moist but not too sticky and starts to pull away from the bowl. If it feels dry, add more water; if it feels too moist, add a dusting of flour.

3 Rub your hands with some oil and bring the dough together into a ball. Cover the bowl with plastic wrap and let rise for 1 hour.

4 MEANWHILE, MAKE THE FILLING: In a large bowl, combine the onion, parsley, ground beef, tomato paste, passata, pomegranate molasses, pepper, kosher salt, curry powder, allspice, and cinnamon. Mix well using your hands until the ingredients are incorporated.

5 Preheat the oven to 450°F (230°C) on the bake setting. If you have one, place a pizza stone on the bottom rack to heat up; otherwise, line a large sheet pan with parchment paper (no need to preheat the sheet pan).

CONTINUED ▶

6 Once the dough has risen, cut it into 6 equal-size pieces and roll each piece into a ball.

7 Lightly sprinkle some flour on your work surface and, using a rolling pin, roll out one of the dough balls into a thin circle (the size does not matter and can be to your preference). Gently remove the dough from the work surface and place it either on a pizza peel lined with parchment paper, if you are using a pizza stone, or on the parchment-lined sheet pan. Place 3 or 4 spoonfuls of the filling on the rolled-out dough, smoothing it out using a spoon to cover the surface with a thin layer, leaving roughly a ¼-inch (6 mm) border.

8 Bake for 7 to 10 minutes, until the bottom is lightly golden. Switch the oven to broil at 500°F (260°C) and broil for 1 to 2 minutes, until the beef has browned. Remove from the oven and transfer it to a large tray, covering it with a kitchen towel or aluminum foil to keep it moist. Reduce the oven heat back to 450°F (230°C) on the bake setting. Repeat steps 7 and 8 with the remaining dough balls and filling. You can stack the lahm bi ajeen pieces over one another in the tray, keeping them covered with a towel.

9 Serve warm or at room temperature. To eat, squeeze the lemon wedges over the surface. Dust the onion slices with the sumac and sprinkle them on top with some chopped parsley; roll up the flatbread to enjoy.

Note

To make this dish quickly without homemade dough, simply use the filling and spread it out on thin tortillas. Reduce the baking time to 5 to 7 minutes and enjoy as instructed in step 9.

Puff Pastry Cheese Fatayer

YIELD: 15 pieces

PREP TIME: 15 minutes, plus 1 hour thawing

COOK TIME: 20 minutes

◇◇◇◇◇

14 ounces (400 g) frozen puff pastry

4½ ounces (130 g) feta cheese, crumbled

4½ ounces (130 g) mozzarella cheese, shredded

4½ ounces (130 g) cream cheese, at room temperature

1 teaspoon dried mint

2 teaspoons dried parsley (or substitute 2 tablespoons finely chopped fresh parsley)

½ teaspoon dried dill

1½ teaspoons ground Aleppo pepper (or substitute paprika)

All-purpose flour, for dusting (optional)

1 large egg, beaten

2 tablespoons white sesame seeds

2 tablespoons nigella seeds

Note

These fatayer can be frozen after baking and cooling. Place them side by side in a freezer bag or airtight container and freeze for up to 2 months. Reheat in the oven and serve warm.

Fatayer are savory pies that are commonly served as appetizers for big dinners or as a light snack in the Middle East. They can be stuffed with cheese, meat, or a tangy spinach stuffing. Typically, they are made with yeast-leavened dough, but I love making them with store-bought puff pastry, which makes the process much quicker. The cheese mixture is made using three types of cheese and flavored with herbs. This recipe is often a go-to when I am hosting a dinner and would like a side dish that's quick to prepare. Make sure you don't skip the sprinkling of sesame and nigella seeds—not only do they look beautiful, but they elevate the flavor too.

1 Bring the puff pastry to room temperature by thawing on the counter for 1 hour.

2 Preheat the oven to 400°F (205°C). Line a large, rimmed sheet pan with parchment paper.

3 In a medium bowl, mix the feta, mozzarella, cream cheese, mint, parsley, dill, and Aleppo pepper until well combined.

4 If using puff pastry that is not precut into squares and must be rolled out, lightly flour your work surface. Using a rolling pin, roll out the pastry until it is ⅛ inch (6 mm) thick. Cut into 4 x 4-inch (10 x 10 cm) squares.

5 Place roughly 1½ tablespoons of the filling on the center of one of the puff pastry squares, gently spreading it out along the diagonal, leaving a ½-inch (13 mm) border. Fold one corner of the square over the filling, diagonally, and pinch it closed at the opposite corner, forming a triangle. Use a fork to press down the open edges until sealed. Transfer to the prepared sheet pan. Repeat with the remaining filling and puff pastry squares. Brush the tops of the fatayer with the beaten egg, then sprinkle them with the sesame and nigella seeds.

6 Bake for 15 to 20 minutes, until the pastry is puffed and golden. You may broil them for 1 to 2 minutes to get more color.

7 Serve warm.

Roasted Eggplant with Labneh

YIELD: 4 to 6 servings
PREP TIME: 10 minutes
COOK TIME: 45 minutes

◇◇◇◇◇

EGGPLANT

2 large eggplants (about 2 pounds,
    or 907 g), ends trimmed, peeled
    lengthwise every other stripe in
    a zebra pattern, and cut into
    ¼-inch-thick (6 mm) rounds
¼ cup plus 1 tablespoon (75 ml)
    olive oil
1 teaspoon kosher salt
2 teaspoons sumac

LABNEH

¾ cup (175 g) Labneh (page 29)
½ teaspoon sumac
2 tablespoons finely chopped fresh
    dill (optional)

FOR GARNISHING AND SERVING

2 tablespoons pine nuts
2 tablespoons roughly torn fresh dill
Pita bread

GARLIC OIL

2 tablespoons olive oil
4 large cloves garlic, thinly sliced
½ teaspoon ground Aleppo
    pepper (or substitute with
    ¼ teaspoon chili flakes)

Eggplant is one of the most beloved vegetables across the Middle East, mainly due to it thriving in the warm climate of the region. It is prepared in countless ways: grilled, fried, roasted, stewed, and stuffed. In Iraq, a plate of fried eggplant is considered a staple at dinnertime, rolled into sandwiches with sliced tomatoes and caramelized onions. People use it as an economical way to replace meat in many dishes because it adds depth, substance, and flavor. I have been an avid fan since I was very little. I still recall my mom being puzzled by the fact that I would devour any eggplant dish placed in front of me, while both of my sisters would turn up their noses. My dad is known for making one eggplant dish in particular, in which he fries it in oil with sliced onions, then he layers yogurt on top and digs in with bread. This dish is reminiscent of that, but using labneh as a base and layering perfectly roasted eggplant seasoned with sumac and dill. The final—and most essential—component is hot garlic oil drizzled on top.

1 TO MAKE THE EGGPLANT: Preheat the oven to 450°F (230°C) and place a rack in the middle.

2 Line two large, rimmed sheet pans with parchment paper and place the eggplant rounds on the pans in a single layer. Drizzle with the oil, then sprinkle with the salt and 2 teaspoons sumac. Mix well to coat all the rounds.

3 Bake for 45 minutes, or until the eggplant is soft and golden.

4 MEANWHILE, PREPARE THE LABNEH: In a small bowl, mix the labneh, ½ teaspoon sumac, and dill (if using) until well combined.

5 TO MAKE THE GARNISH: Toast the pine nuts in a small, dry skillet over medium heat for a few minutes, or until lightly golden, stirring continuously. Transfer to a small bowl.

6 WHEN THE EGGPLANT IS BAKED AND JUST BEFORE SERVING, MAKE THE GARLIC OIL: In the same skillet the pine nuts were toasted in, heat the olive oil over medium heat. Add the garlic and cook, stirring continuously, for a few minutes, or until sizzling and golden. Stir in the Aleppo pepper and remove from the heat.

7 Spread the labneh onto a medium serving platter and top with the roasted eggplant rounds. Spoon the garlic oil evenly over the top, then garnish with the toasted pine nuts and fresh dill. Serve with pita bread.

Lebanese Batata Harra
BAKED SPICY POTATOES

YIELD: 6 servings

PREP TIME: 10 minutes

COOK TIME: 35 minutes

◇◇◇◇◇

4 large yellow potatoes (about 2¼ pounds, or 1 kg), peeled, washed, patted dry, and cut into 1½-inch-long x ½-inch-thick (4 x 1.3 cm) pieces

4 tablespoons (60 ml) olive oil, divided

1 teaspoon paprika

1 teaspoon kosher salt

½ teaspoon ground coriander

6 large cloves garlic, minced

½ teaspoon chili flakes

FOR GARNISHING AND SERVING

¼ cup (13 g) finely chopped fresh parsley or cilantro

Juice of ½ lemon

Chili flakes

Who doesn't love a side of crispy potatoes? But this recipe has you skipping the bland seasoning and spicing them up, Lebanese-style. Batata harra is a common mezze dish served as an appetizer at Lebanese restaurants. Some versions are spicier than others, so I will leave the spice level for you to decide by adding more or less chili flakes. These are best enjoyed straight out of the pan, and I often struggle to get a full portion over to the dinner table!

1 Preheat the oven to 450°F (230°C) and place a rack on the bottom.

2 Line a large, rimmed sheet pan with parchment paper and place the potatoes in the pan in a single layer. Drizzle with 2 tablespoons of the oil, then sprinkle with the paprika, salt, and coriander.

3 Bake for 25 minutes, then remove the pan from the oven and flip the potatoes. Place the pan back into the oven and bake for 10 to 15 minutes longer, until the potatoes are crispy.

4 In a small skillet, heat the remaining 2 tablespoons oil over medium heat. Add the garlic and chili flakes and cook, stirring continuously, for 1 minute, or until the garlic is golden and fragrant.

5 Pour the hot oil over the baked potatoes and toss to combine.

6 Garnish with the chopped parsley or cilantro, a squeeze of lemon, and more chili flakes. Serve immediately.

Main Dishes
30 Minutes

Sheet-Pan Chicken Shawarma

YIELD: 6 servings

PREP TIME: 10 minutes, plus 1 hour marinating

COOK TIME: 15 minutes

◇◇◇◇◇

2 teaspoons ground cumin

2 teaspoons paprika

1 teaspoon ground allspice

1 teaspoon ground cinnamon

½ teaspoon ground cloves

½ teaspoon ground cardamom

¼ teaspoon cayenne pepper

1 teaspoon kosher salt

Juice of ½ lemon

4 tablespoons olive oil, divided

1⅔ pounds (750 g) boneless, skinless chicken thighs (about 7 large thighs)

1 large yellow onion, thinly sliced

2 large cloves garlic, minced

FOR SERVING (OPTIONAL)

Toum (page 22)

Saj or pita bread

Assorted vegetables (such as sliced cucumber, sliced tomato, shredded lettuce, and sliced pickles)

Roz Asfar (page 71)

Salata (page 44)

Quite possibly the dish that has for so long defined Middle Eastern cuisine, chicken shawarma has a special place in every Arab household. Although so much of my work goes into showing people that there is a plethora of vibrant Middle Eastern recipes beyond just shawarma, I will never deny the true satisfaction a shawarma wrap smothered in Toum (page 22) brings. Over the years, I have tweaked and perfected my shawarma marinade and cooking technique, optimizing for both efficiency and flavor. I've arrived at a few conclusions. Chicken thighs are the best cut of chicken to use to maintain moist and fatty shawarma. Also, the best way to cook large quantities quickly is using a pre-oiled and preheated sheet pan; spread the chicken out over the hot sheet pan, and twenty minutes later, you'll have perfectly moist and tender chicken with dark crispy bits throughout. The most authentic way to enjoy shawarma is wrapped in Saj bread, a very thin flatbread. Smother the bread with toum, add the shawarma, followed by some pickles and french fries (yes, fries!), and then wrap it up and take a bite.

1 In a large bowl, combine the cumin, paprika, allspice, cinnamon, cloves, cardamom, cayenne, and salt. Add the lemon juice and 1 tablespoon of the oil and mix to create a paste.

2 Trim any excess fat from the chicken thighs, then cut them into thin strips, roughly ¼ to ½ inch (6 to 13 mm) wide.

3 Add the chicken, onion, and garlic to the marinade and mix well. Cover the bowl with plastic wrap and marinate in the refrigerator for 1 to 4 hours. (If you are short on time, you can use it right away.)

4 When ready to cook the shawarma, preheat the oven to 450°F (230°C).

5 Place the remaining 3 tablespoons oil on a large, rimmed sheet pan and spread it evenly. Heat the oiled sheet pan for 5 to 7 minutes in the preheated oven.

6 Carefully place the chicken in a single layer on the hot baking sheet and bake for 15 to 20 minutes, until fully cooked through. (Check that the chicken is white on the inside and the juices run clear.) The chicken should look charred and browned on the outside. You can broil for a few more minutes if you want additional color on the chicken.

7 Serve with toum, bread, and assorted vegetables to make wraps, or alongside rice and salad.

Lebanese Shish Tawook

CHICKEN SKEWERS

YIELD: 7 to 10 skewers

PREP TIME: 10 minutes, plus 1 hour marinating

COOK TIME: 20 minutes

◇◇◇◇◇

7 to 10 metal or bamboo skewers

¾ cup (180 ml) plain, whole-milk yogurt

2 tablespoons tomato paste

3 tablespoons olive oil

5 cloves garlic, minced

Juice of 1 large lemon

1 teaspoon kosher salt

1 teaspoon paprika

½ teaspoon ground cinnamon

½ teaspoon ground ginger

2 teaspoons onion powder

¼ teaspoon black pepper

4 chicken breasts (about 1½ pounds, or 700 g), cut into 2-inch (5 cm) cubes

Olive oil, for greasing (optional)

FOR SERVING

½ medium red onion, sliced

1 tablespoon sumac

Assorted vegetables (such as sliced cucumber, sliced tomato, shredded lettuce, and sliced pickles)

Pita bread

Toum (page 22) or Tarator (page 30)

Shish tawook, although popularized as a classic Lebanese grilled chicken dish, actually gets its name from Turkish origins. The word *shish* comes from the Turkish word *şiş*, meaning "skewer," and the word *tawook* comes from the Turkish word *tavuk*, meaning "chicken." Grilled chicken skewers are another universal dish across the Middle East. In Iraq we call it chicken "tikka," a word from Indian origin, and season it with more Eastern spices. The Lebanese marinade, which I make quite often, has a mix of tomato paste, yogurt, garlic, and lemon juice as the base, along with a few spices. These ingredients yield tender, juicy, and mild-flavored chicken, perfect for rolling into pita wraps. Although the skewers are typically grilled outdoors, don't let winter stop you from enjoying it; it is perfectly delicious grilled on an indoor cast-iron pan. As with many Lebanese chicken dishes, it is often served with Toum (page 22) or Tarator (page 30).

1 If using bamboo skewers for this recipe, start by soaking them in water for 15 minutes.

2 In a large bowl, mix together the yogurt, tomato paste, oil, garlic, lemon juice, salt, paprika, cinnamon, ginger, onion powder, and pepper until well combined.

3 Add the chicken cubes to the marinade and mix until all the chicken is thoroughly coated. Cover the bowl with plastic wrap and let the meat marinate in the refrigerator for at least 1 hour, or preferably overnight. Take out 30 minutes before cooking to bring the chicken to room temperature.

4 Skewer the marinated chicken cubes onto the skewers, using roughly 4 or 5 pieces per skewer, depending on the size of the skewers.

5 Meanwhile, preheat an outdoor grill to 400°F (205°C). If grilling indoors, preheat a large cast-iron grill pan over medium heat and grease it with oil.

6 Grill the skewers for 5 to 6 minutes per side, ensuring the chicken is white and cooked through on the inside and golden on the outside. Avoid grilling the chicken for too long or it will dry out.

7 Dust the onion slices with the sumac and serve alongside the skewers, assorted vegetables, pita bread, and toum or tarator to make wraps.

One-Pot Chicken & Saffron Orzo

YIELD: 4 or 5 servings
PREP TIME: 10 minutes
COOK TIME: 20 minutes

◇◇◇◇◇

CHICKEN

1½ pounds (680 g) boneless, skinless chicken breasts (about 4 large breasts)
1 teaspoon kosher salt
1 teaspoon onion powder
1 teaspoon garlic powder
1 teaspoon parsley flakes
1 teaspoon paprika
½ teaspoon black pepper
1 tablespoon olive oil
1 tablespoon butter

ORZO

½ teaspoon saffron strands
2 tablespoons hot water
1 tablespoon olive oil
½ large yellow onion, finely chopped
1 teaspoon kosher salt
½ teaspoon onion powder
½ teaspoon garlic powder
¼ teaspoon paprika
2 large cloves garlic, minced
16 ounces (454 g) orzo
4 cups (960 ml) chicken broth
1 tablespoon butter

FOR GARNISHING AND SERVING

¼ cup (13 g) finely chopped fresh parsley
Lemon slices
Salata (page 44) or Arugula & Pomegranate Salad (page 52)

If it's not already evident by the number of rice recipes in this cookbook, I cook rice a lot. But when I want a pleasant change, one of my favorite carbs to cook is orzo. It absorbs flavor like a sponge, and when cooked with the right liquid ratio, it can be silky smooth and pleasant to eat.

1 TO MAKE THE CHICKEN: Place a chicken breast on a cutting board and hold it flat with the palm of your non-knife-holding hand. Using a sharp chef's knife, slice the chicken breast horizontally into 2 even cutlets using as few strokes as possible for a smooth finish. Repeat with the remaining chicken breasts.

2 In a large bowl, mix together the salt, 1 teaspoon onion powder, 1 teaspoon garlic powder, parsley flakes, 1 teaspoon paprika, and pepper. Add the chicken cutlets and thoroughly coat with the seasoning mix.

3 In a large 2-inch-deep (5 cm) skillet, heat the oil and butter over medium heat. Add the chicken cutlets, working in batches so as to avoid overcrowding, and sear for 2 minutes on each side until golden. Transfer to a plate.

4 TO MAKE THE ORZO: Bloom the saffron by grinding the strands into a powder using a mortar and pestle. Place the powder in a small bowl, pour in the hot water, and let sit for 5 minutes.

5 In the same skillet the chicken was cooked in, heat the oil over medium heat. Add the onion and cook, stirring often, for 5 minutes, or until softened and translucent. Add the salt, ½ teaspoon onion powder, ½ teaspoon garlic powder, ¼ teaspoon paprika, and garlic and cook, stirring often, for a few more minutes. Add the orzo and toast it for a few minutes, stirring continuously. Stir in the broth and saffron water and bring to a boil.

6 Once boiling, add the chicken cutlets back into the skillet in a single layer, cover the skillet with a tight-fitting lid, and cook over medium heat for 5 minutes. Turn off the heat and let sit for 10 minutes. Check that the chicken cutlets are cooked through by using a meat thermometer and ensuring the interior is heated to 165°F (74°C), or by cutting a piece to check that it is white inside. If required, cover and cook for a few more minutes.

7 Cut the 1 tablespoon butter into small pieces and add it over the orzo to finish, then garnish with the chopped parsley and a squeeze of lemon. Serve with salad.

Lebanese Tahini Chicken

YIELD: 4 servings
PREP TIME: 10 minutes
COOK TIME: 20 minutes

◇◇◇◇◇

CHICKEN

1½ pounds (650 g) boneless, skinless chicken breasts (3 large breasts; or substitute boneless chicken thighs), cut into 1-inch (2.5 cm) cubes

1 teaspoon kosher salt

1 teaspoon paprika

½ teaspoon black pepper

1 teaspoon ground allspice

1 teaspoon onion powder

1 teaspoon garlic powder

3 tablespoons olive oil, divided

TAHINI SAUCE

½ cup (90 ml) fresh lemon juice, plus more if needed

½ cup (120 ml) tahini

1 cup (240 ml) plain, whole-milk yogurt

7 large cloves garlic, minced

1½ teaspoons kosher salt, plus more if needed

½ teaspoon black pepper

1 teaspoon garlic powder

1 teaspoon onion powder

FOR GARNISHING AND SERVING

1 tablespoon olive oil

½ cup whole cashews (60 g), slivered almonds (55 g), or pine nuts (65 g)

½ cup (25 g) finely chopped fresh parsley

Roz Asfar (page 71) or
 Roz Bi Shaariya (page 67)

Salata (page 44)

In Levantine cuisine, a lemony tahini sauce makes its way into many dishes, both as a cold sauce drizzled on falafel and shawarma and as a simmer sauce in hot dishes, typically with fish, or kofta. This recipe is a secret weapon on busy weeknights, typically ready within thirty minutes. Boneless chicken breast pieces are seasoned and seared, then simmered for a few minutes in a tangy and zingy tahini, garlic, and yogurt sauce. And do not skip the final finishing touches: the crunchy toasted nuts and a sprinkling of parsley really do deliver the last element of texture and freshness.

1 TO MAKE THE CHICKEN: In a large bowl, mix the chicken with the 1 teaspoon salt, paprika, pepper, allspice, onion powder, garlic powder, and 1 tablespoon of the oil until well combined. Set aside.

2 TO MAKE THE TAHINI SAUCE: In a medium bowl, whisk together the lemon juice, tahini, yogurt, garlic, 1½ teaspoons salt, pepper, garlic powder, and onion powder with ½ cup (120 ml) of water until the consistency is smooth.

3 In a large skillet, heat the remaining 2 tablespoons olive oil over medium heat for 2 minutes. Add the chicken and sear it for 2 minutes on each side, or until lightly golden, working in batches to avoid overcrowding. Transfer to a plate. The chicken does not need to be fully cooked, as it will simmer in the sauce.

4 Place all the chicken back into the skillet, then pour the tahini sauce on top. Let the chicken and sauce simmer for 5 to 7 minutes, until the sauce is bubbling and the chicken is fully white on the inside. Taste and adjust for salt and/or lemon juice if needed.

5 MEANWHILE, MAKE THE GARNISH: Heat the 1 tablespoon oil in a small skillet over low heat, then add the nuts and toast for 5 minutes, or until golden, stirring often.

6 Garnish with the chopped parsley and toasted nuts and serve with rice and salad.

Baked Moroccan Chermoula Meatballs with Couscous

YIELD: 18 meatballs; 4 to 6 servings

PREP TIME: 10 minutes

COOK TIME: 15 minutes

◇◇◇◇◇

MEATBALLS

1 pound (454 g) lean ground beef

1 large egg

¼ cup (25 g) bread crumbs

½ teaspoon kosher salt

2 tablespoons paprika

2 tablespoons olive oil, plus more
   for greasing

¼ cup (60 g) Moroccan Chermoula
   (page 26)

COUSCOUS

1 cup (195 g) couscous

½ teaspoon kosher salt, plus more
   to taste

1 cup (240 ml) boiling water

2 tablespoons olive oil

2 tablespoons Moroccan Chermoula
   (page 26)

FOR GARNISHING AND SERVING

¼ cup slivered almonds (30 g)
   or pine nuts (35 g)

Salata (page 44) or Arugula &
   Pomegranate Salad (page 52)

This recipe has a special place in my heart, because it combines two things I love: baked meatballs (one of the quickest meals to make) and Moroccan Chermoula (page 26). This is the perfect way to elevate boring meatballs into a sophisticated, weeknight-friendly meal and to show just how versatile chermoula is. By no means is this a traditional recipe—it came about as a result of my tinkering with leftovers from my fridge one day. Using chermoula in the meatballs gives them just the right amount of flavor and moisture to keep them juicy, and while they bake in the oven, you can quickly make the couscous, which also gets a few dollops of chermoula stirred through it. This meal is best enjoyed with a citrusy side salad.

1 Preheat the oven to 425°F (220°C).

2 TO MAKE THE MEATBALLS: In a large bowl, combine the ground beef, egg, bread crumbs, salt, paprika, oil, and ¼ cup (60 g) chermoula and mix well using your hands.

3 Roll the meat mixture into even-size balls, roughly 1½ inches (4 cm) in diameter. Place the meatballs in a single layer on a large, rimmed sheet pan that has been lightly coated with olive oil.

4 Bake for 10 to 12 minutes, until browned on the outside and fully cooked on the inside. Avoid baking too long to keep them moist.

5 WHILE THE MEATBALLS ARE BAKING, PREPARE THE COUSCOUS: Place the couscous in a medium bowl and mix with the salt. Add the boiling water, then cover the bowl with a lid or a large plate and allow the couscous to absorb the water for 10 minutes.

6 TO MAKE THE GARNISH: In a small, dry skillet, toast the almonds over medium heat for 5 to 6 minutes, until lightly golden, stirring continuously.

7 Uncover the couscous, then add the olive oil and 2 tablespoons chermoula and mix thoroughly. Taste and adjust for salt. Mix in 2 tablespoons of the toasted almonds, reserving the rest for garnish.

8 Garnish the meatballs with the toasted almonds, drizzle with more chermoula, and serve with the couscous and salad.

Deconstructed Turkish Manti

YIELD: 6 servings
PREP TIME: 15 minutes
COOK TIME: 20 minutes

◇◇◇◇◇

PASTA
1 tablespoon kosher salt
16 ounces (454 g) farfalle or conchiglie (shell) pasta
1 tablespoon olive oil

MEAT MIXTURE
2 tablespoons olive oil
1 large onion, finely chopped
1½ pounds (680 g) lean ground beef
3 large cloves garlic, minced
3 tablespoons tomato paste
1¼ teaspoons kosher salt
¼ teaspoon cayenne pepper
1½ teaspoons paprika

YOGURT SAUCE
3 cups (720 ml) plain, whole-milk yogurt
1 large clove garlic, minced
⅛ teaspoon black pepper
¼ teaspoon kosher salt
1½ teaspoons dried mint

TOASTED ALMONDS
2 teaspoons olive oil
½ cup (55 g) slivered almonds

CHILI BUTTER
2 tablespoons salted butter, melted
1 teaspoons ground Aleppo pepper (or substitute with ½ teaspoon chili flakes)

FOR GARNISHING
Dried mint
Aleppo pepper (or substitute with chili flakes)

Manti is an iconic Turkish dish made of dumplings filled with seasoned beef, dunked into a savory yogurt sauce, and finished with a drizzle of chili butter. This type of dish is quite common across other countries, resembling the Levantine *shish barak* and the Afghan *mantu*. It's my usual order at my local Turkish restaurant—delicious, comforting, and full of texture. But I had to find a shortcut, as the authentic dish requires hand-shaping tiny dumplings using made-from-scratch dough. Instead, I use pasta to instantly transform this dish into a weeknight-friendly meal.

1 TO MAKE THE PASTA: Fill a large pot with cold water, add the 1 tablespoon salt, and bring to a boil over medium-high heat. Add the pasta and cook according to the package instructions for al dente. Reserve ½ cup (120 ml) of the pasta cooking water, then drain the pasta and coat it with the 1 tablespoon oil to prevent it from sticking.

2 MEANWHILE, MAKE THE MEAT MIXTURE: In a large skillet, heat the 2 tablespoons oil over medium-high heat for 1 to 2 minutes. Add the onion and cook, stirring occasionally, for 4 to 5 minutes, until softened and translucent. Add the ground beef and cook, breaking it up into small pieces with a wooden spoon, for 7 to 10 minutes, until browned. Add the 3 cloves minced garlic, tomato paste, 1¼ teaspoons salt, cayenne, and paprika to the skillet. Mix well and cook for 1 to 2 minutes. Turn off the heat.

3 TO MAKE THE YOGURT SAUCE: In a medium bowl, whisk together the yogurt, 1 clove minced garlic, black pepper, ¼ teaspoon salt, and mint with 4 or 5 tablespoons of the reserved pasta cooking water until a smooth sauce forms.

4 TO TOAST THE ALMONDS: Heat the 2 teaspoons oil in a small skillet over low heat, then add the slivered almonds and toast for 2 to 3 minutes, until golden, stirring often. Transfer to a small bowl.

5 TO MAKE THE CHILI BUTTER: In the same small skillet the almonds were toasted in, melt the butter over medium heat. Add the Aleppo pepper and cook, stirring continuously, for 30 seconds. Remove from the heat.

6 Spread the cooked pasta in a layer on a serving dish. Spoon the meat mixture over it and drizzle with the yogurt sauce and chili butter. Garnish with dried mint, toasted almonds, and Aleppo pepper. Serve immediately.

Turkish Lamb Chops

YIELD: 4 servings

PREP TIME: 5 minutes, plus 1 hour marinating

COOK TIME: 25 minutes

◇◇◇◇◇

12 lamb rib chops (about 2¼ pounds, or 1 kg) (or substitute loin chops)

¼ cup (60 ml) fresh lemon juice (about 2 lemons)

¼ cup (60 ml) plus 2 tablespoons olive oil, divided

1 teaspoon ground Aleppo pepper (or substitute with ¼ teaspoon chili flakes)

½ teaspoon ground cumin

½ teaspoon ground coriander

1 teaspoon dried oregano

1½ teaspoons kosher salt

2 tablespoons sweet red pepper paste (or substitute tomato paste)

FOR SERVING

Turkish Bulgur Pilaf (page 64)

Salata (page 44)

Yogurt

The preferred choice of protein in Iraq and across most of the Middle East is lamb. I grew up loving the smell and taste of lamb, so much so that when I realized some people don't like how it smells and tastes, I was shocked! Lamb represents the protein of kings for us, and it's served to guests as a way of honoring them. I find that lamb chops are probably the most accessible cut of lamb that almost everyone will love; they are known for their tenderness, succulence, and rich flavor. I would be happy to eat lamb chops simply seasoned with salt and pepper, but this Turkish-style marinade is easy to throw together and really elevates the chops. I serve them with a side of Turkish Bulgur Pilaf (page 64) and a salad.

1 In a large bowl, mix the lamb chops with the lemon juice, ¼ cup (60 ml) of the oil, Aleppo pepper, cumin, coriander, oregano, salt, and red pepper paste until well combined.

2 Cover the bowl with plastic wrap and let the lamb chops marinate in the refrigerator for at least 1 hour, or overnight. Let come to room temperature for at least 30 minutes before cooking them.

3 Heat a large cast-iron pan over medium heat. Add the remaining 2 tablespoons oil. Working in batches, add the lamb chops to the pan and cook for 2 to 3 minutes on each side for medium doneness.

4 Transfer the cooked chops to a plate and cover with aluminum foil. Let rest for 10 minutes before serving.

5 Serve the lamb chops over the bulgur pilaf with salad and yogurt.

One-Pot Shrimp & Rice

YIELD: 4 servings

PREP TIME: 5 minutes

COOK TIME: 25 minutes

◇◇◇◇◇

SEASONING

1½ teaspoons kosher salt

1½ teaspoons onion powder

1½ teaspoons ground coriander

1 teaspoon ground turmeric

1 teaspoon ground allspice

1 teaspoon paprika

½ teaspoon black pepper

½ teaspoon ground cumin

½ teaspoon ground cinnamon

SHRIMP

2 pounds (900 g) large or jumbo
   shrimp, peeled, deveined, and
   patted dry

1 tablespoon olive oil

RICE

¼ cup (60 ml) vegetable oil

1 small onion, finely chopped

3 cloves garlic, minced

2 cups (360 g) long-grain white
   basmati rice, rinsed until the water
   runs clear and drained completely

2 cups (270 g) frozen peas

3½ cups (840 ml) chicken broth

½ teaspoon kosher salt

FOR GARNISHING AND SERVING

Finely chopped fresh parsley

Fresh lemon juice

Salata (page 44)

It's no secret why one-pot meals are so popular: you get all the components of a well-balanced meal cooked up in one pot. I whip up this dish quite frequently on busy weeknights involving a lot of mom duties, and since my kids are huge fans of shrimp, it's a dream. The shrimp is coated in a blend of warm Middle Eastern spices and cooked for just a few minutes before being removed. Once the rice is cooked in the same pot and ready to be steamed into its final fluffy form, the shrimp is added back in to finish cooking. This method guarantees extra-plump and -juicy shrimp.

1 TO MAKE THE SEASONING: In a small bowl, mix all the seasoning ingredients until well combined.

2 TO MAKE THE SHRIMP: Place the shrimp in a small bowl and mix them with half of the seasoning mixture.

3 In a 4½-quart (4.3 L) sauté pan with a tight-fitting lid, heat the olive oil over medium heat. Add the shrimp and cook for 30 seconds on each side, working in batches to avoid overcrowding. Transfer to a plate.

4 TO MAKE THE RICE: In the same pan the shrimp were cooked in, over medium heat, add the vegetable oil and the onion and cook, stirring occasionally, for 4 to 5 minutes, until softened and translucent. Add the garlic and the remaining seasoning mixture and cook, stirring often, for a few more minutes, or until fragrant.

5 Add the rice and mix well. Add the frozen peas, followed by the broth. Season with the ½ teaspoon salt and bring to a boil. Once boiling, cover the pot with the lid, reduce the heat to low, and let cook for 20 minutes.

6 Turn off the heat and fluff the rice with a fork. Add the shrimp back into the pan on top of the rice. Cover again with the lid and let stand for 10 minutes.

7 Garnish with parsley and a squeeze of lemon juice. Serve with salad.

Harissa Honey Shrimp Skewers

YIELD: 4 to 6 servings

PREP TIME: 15 minutes, plus 15 minutes marinating

COOK TIME: 15 minutes

◇◇◇◇◇

6 to 8 bamboo or metal skewers

¼ cup (90 g) Tunisian Harissa (page 25)

¼ cup (60 ml) honey

1 tablespoon olive oil, plus more for greasing if needed

1 teaspoon kosher salt

1½ pounds (680 g) large shrimp (20 to 30 shrimp), peeled, deveined, and patted dry

3 small yellow onions, cut into quarters

FOR GARNISHING AND SERVING

½ cup (25 g) finely chopped fresh parsley

Tunisian Harissa (page 25)

Note

You may also cook the shrimp on a grill pan on the stovetop without skewering them. Cook them over medium heat for 1 minute per side, or until they curl and look opaque. You can serve alongside the Arugula & Pomegranate Salad (page 52) or Tahini Cabbage Slaw (page 48). The shrimp are also delicious in wraps with the slaw.

Having a jar of Tunisian Harissa (page 25) in your fridge means you can have a fancy meal on the dinner table in twenty minutes. A big part of the solution is also shrimp, the quickest-cooking protein! The marinade for these shrimp skewers couldn't be simpler, because the work is already done for you with the harissa paste. I love mixing harissa with honey to balance the spiciness and help caramelize the shrimp. Use an indoor or outdoor grill, and while you're at it, toss some onions in the marinade and throw them on the grill too. They'll soften and become sweeter—and the perfect accompaniment to the shrimp.

1 If using bamboo skewers for this recipe, start by soaking them in water for 15 minutes.

2 In a large bowl, mix the harissa, honey, oil, and salt until well combined. Add the shrimp to the bowl and mix well, ensuring all the shrimp are coated. Let the shrimp marinate in the refrigerator for 15 minutes.

3 Remove the shrimp from the fridge and skewer them, 4 or 5 shrimp per skewer, then place on a platter and let come to room temperature for 10 minutes. Reserve the leftover marinade. Toss the quartered onions in the bowl of leftover marinade to soak it up, then place them on the remaining skewers.

4 Meanwhile, preheat an outdoor grill to 400°F (205°C). If grilling indoors, preheat a large cast-iron grill pan over medium heat. Grease the grill pan with oil to avoid the shrimp sticking.

5 If grilling outdoors, grill the skewers over direct, medium heat for 5 to 6 minutes, turning the shrimp halfway through, until the shrimp curl and turn opaque. If grilling indoors, place the skewers on the grill pan and cook for 1 minute per side, or until the shrimp curl and turn opaque. Grill the onion skewers for 3 to 4 minutes per side, until charred and softened.

6 Place the skewers on a platter along with the grilled onions and garnish with the chopped parsley. Serve more harissa in a bowl for dipping.

Pomegranate Salmon Bites with Tahini Kale Salad

YIELD: 4 servings

PREP TIME: 10 minutes

COOK TIME: 20 minutes

◇◇◇◇◇

SALMON BITES

4 tablespoons pomegranate molasses, divided

2 tablespoons honey

2 large cloves garlic, minced

1 teaspoon chili flakes

1½ tablespoons olive oil, divided

½ teaspoon kosher salt

1⅓ pounds (600 g) skinless salmon fillets, cut into 1-inch (2.5 cm) cubes

SUMAC PITA CHIPS

1 pita bread (8 inches, or 20 cm), cut into 1-inch (2.5 cm) squares

1 tablespoon olive oil

1 tablespoon sumac

¼ teaspoon kosher salt

KALE CAESAR SALAD

¼ cup (60 ml) tahini

2 tablespoons fresh lemon juice

1 small clove garlic, crushed

1 tablespoon Dijon mustard

1 tablespoon mayonnaise

½ teaspoon kosher salt

⅛ teaspoon black pepper

5¼ ounces (150 g kale), roughly chopped or torn into bite-size pieces

1 tablespoon olive oil

¼ cup (25 g) grated or shaved Parmesan cheese

I cook with salmon quite often, mainly because it cooks quickly, reserving it for nights when I don't have much time to get dinner on the table. Salmon bites cook even quicker than a large fillet, and they're fun for my kids to eat. The tartness from the pomegranate molasses in the marinade cuts through the richness of the salmon perfectly. I serve this dish with a kale Caesar salad, but Middle Eastern–style, with a tahini Caesar dressing and pita chips.

1 Preheat the oven to 400°F (205°C) and place a rack on the bottom.

2 TO MAKE THE SALMON BITES: In a medium bowl, mix together 3 tablespoons of the pomegranate molasses, the honey, minced garlic, chili flakes, 1 tablespoon of the oil, and the ½ teaspoon salt. Add the salmon cubes to the bowl and thoroughly coat with the marinade. Let marinate for 10 minutes.

3 MEANWHILE, MAKE THE SUMAC PITA CHIPS: Place the pita squares on a large baking sheet in a single layer. Drizzle with the 1 tablespoon oil, then sprinkle with the sumac and ¼ teaspoon salt. Mix well and place on the bottom rack in the oven. Bake for 5 to 7 minutes, until golden. Keep an eye on them, as they tend to burn quickly.

4 In a large skillet, heat the remaining ½ tablespoon oil over medium heat for a few minutes. Add the salmon bites, working in batches to avoid overcrowding, and sear for 1 to 2 minutes per side, until golden. Transfer to a plate.

5 TO MAKE THE KALE CAESAR SALAD: In a small bowl, whisk together the tahini, lemon juice, crushed garlic, Dijon, mayonnaise, ½ teaspoon salt, and pepper for the dressing. Use 2 or 3 tablespoons of water to thin it out to your desired consistency.

6 Add the kale to a large salad bowl, then add the oil and massage it into the kale to soften the fibers. Add the dressing to the bowl and toss to coat the kale. Top with the crispy sumac pita chips and Parmesan.

7 Serve the salmon bites alongside the salad, drizzling the remaining 1 tablespoon pomegranate molasses onto the salmon on each plate, if desired.

Sarra's Saucy Skillet Trout

YIELD: 4 servings

PREP TIME: 10 minutes

COOK TIME: 10 minutes

◇◇◇◇◇

SPICE PASTE

1 teaspoon kosher salt, plus more
   to taste

1½ teaspoons paprika

1 teaspoon ground coriander

1 teaspoon ground cumin

1 teaspoon ground turmeric

2 tablespoons avocado oil

TROUT

1 skin-on rainbow trout fillet
   (1½ pounds, or 680 g), cut into
   4 or 5 pieces

1 tablespoon avocado oil

½ large yellow onion, finely chopped

2 large cloves garlic, minced

½ large red bell pepper, finely
   chopped

1 tablespoon tomato paste

1 tablespoon pomegranate molasses
   (see Note)

1 cup (240 ml) boiling water

GARNISHING AND SERVING

2 tablespoons finely chopped
   fresh parsley

Roz Asfar (page 71)

Salata (page 44)

Note

If you don't have pomegranate molasses, you can substitute it with a few squeezes of lemon juice.

My older sister, Sarra, is an amazing cook, and the one person (aside from my mom) whom I consult quite often regarding cookbook and blog recipes. With her living in the United States and me in Canada, we often call each other and talk for hours on end to catch up and discuss what's for dinner. She gave me this recipe once when I was feeling uninspired. Ever since that day, it has been one of the main ways I make fish, and I keep referring to it as "Sarra's Fish." It's very quick to make, perfectly seasoned with cumin and coriander, and super saucy, for serving alongside rice.

1 TO MAKE THE SPICE PASTE: In a small bowl, combine all the paste ingredients and mix well.

2 TO MAKE THE TROUT: Reserve 1 to 2 teaspoons of the spice paste, then slather the remaining paste all over the trout fillet.

3 In a large nonstick skillet, heat the 1 tablespoon avocado oil over medium-high heat. Add the trout and sear the pieces for 1 minute per side until golden. Transfer to a plate.

4 In the same skillet the trout was cooked in, add the onion, garlic, bell pepper, and reserved spice paste. Cook and stir for 3 to 4 minutes, until the onion is softened.

5 Add the tomato paste and pomegranate molasses and mix until well combined. Pour in the boiling water and stir to create a sauce. Cover the pan with the lid and reduce the heat to medium. Let simmer for 5 to 7 minutes. If you want a thicker sauce, uncover the pan and allow the water to bubble for 3 to 4 minutes to reduce.

6 Add the trout pieces back into the skillet, cover the pan again, and let simmer for 8 to 10 minutes. Check that the fish is cooked by inserting a fork at it thickest part; it should be nearly opaque, moist, and flake easily with the fork.

7 Spoon the pan sauce over the top of the fish and garnish with the chopped parsley. Serve with the rice and salad.

Muhammara Pasta

YIELD: 6 servings
PREP TIME: 10 minutes
COOK TIME: 20 minutes

◇◇◇◇◇

PASTA
Kosher salt
13 ounces (360 g) pasta shape
  of choice
1 cup (20 g) packed baby spinach
½ cup (12 g) packed basil leaves
¼ cup (60 g) sliced Kalamata olives
  (or any other black olives)
½ cup (25 g) shaved Parmesan
  cheese

MUHAMMARA SAUCE
10 ounces (300 g) jarred roasted red
  peppers (about 3 large peppers)
1½ ounces (40 g) sun-dried
  tomatoes
½ cup (50 g) unsalted whole
  raw walnuts
2 large cloves garlic
½ teaspoon kosher salt
1 tablespoon tomato paste
2 tablespoons pomegranate
  molasses
2 tablespoons olive oil
1 teaspoon ground Aleppo pepper
  (or substitute with 1 teaspoon
  paprika)

FOR GARNISHING
Shaved Parmesan cheese
Basil leaves
Black pepper

This dish came to be when I had leftover Syrian Muhammara (page 38) from a dinner gathering and decided to spoon it into cooked pasta in my fridge. It was incredibly tasty, and I knew I had to develop this into a recipe in its own right. I added spinach, basil, black olives, and Parmesan to jazz it up and make it more of a balanced dish, but feel free to add any vegetables you like. We now look forward to this dish the day after I make a batch of muhammara!

1 To make the pasta: Fill a large pot with cold water, add salt, and bring to a boil over medium-high heat. Add the pasta and cook according to the package instructions for al dente.

2 Meanwhile, make the muhammara sauce: Add all the sauce ingredients to a food processor and process for 1 minute until a smooth paste forms.

3 Add the muhammara sauce to a large, deep skillet and cook for 1 to 2 minutes, stirring often.

4 Drain the pasta, reserving 1 cup (240 ml) of pasta cooking water. Add the cooked pasta to the skillet along with the baby spinach, basil leaves, olives, and Parmesan. Mix everything together, then add the reserved pasta cooking water to loosen the sauce.

5 Garnish with more Parmesan, basil leaves, and black pepper. Serve immediately.

Note
This muhammara sauce is almost the same as the muhammara dip on page 38 but without the addition of bread crumbs. If you have leftovers of the muhammara dip, feel free to use it to replace this sauce.

Main Dishes
1 Hour

Libyan Mbakbaka
SPICY CHICKEN PASTA

YIELD: 6 servings
PREP TIME: 10 minutes
COOK TIME: 50 minutes

◇◇◇◇◇

¼ cup (60 g) olive oil

1 medium onion, finely chopped

8 large cloves garlic, minced

3 jalapeño peppers (see Notes), 2 kept whole and 1 finely chopped with seeds

8 chicken drumsticks (about 2 pounds, or 900 g)

2½ teaspoons kosher salt, plus more to taste

½ teaspoon ground turmeric

½ teaspoon black pepper

¼ teaspoon cayenne pepper (optional)

¾ cup (200 g) tomato paste

16 ounces (454 g) ditalini pasta (or substitute penne or conchiglie)

½ cup (25 g) finely chopped fresh parsley, for garnishing

Notes

+ For milder results, discard the seeds before finely chopping the jalapeño.

+ To make this dish vegetarian, skip the drumsticks and use 2 large peeled and diced potatoes and 2 cups (270 g) of frozen peas. Add them in step 2 and use vegetable broth instead of water.

I spent five years of my childhood in Libya and have a deep fondness for Libyan people, for Benghazi (the city we lived in), and for Libyan food. I just had to introduce you to Libyan mbakbaka, which is a spicy pasta dish made with either chicken or red meat and plenty of hot peppers. It's called *mbakbaka* because it is typically served with a lot of liquid, and as this liquid simmers in the final stages of cooking, it creates bubbles and makes a "bak bak bak" sound. The pasta is cooked in the same pot with the chicken, tomato paste, and spices, which helps the pasta absorb the umami from the chicken. Some versions use a common yellow Libyan spice mix called *bzaar*. Some Libyan families add potatoes or peas and carrots to increase the nutritional value.

1 In a medium nonstick pot over medium heat, add the olive oil and heat for 1 to 2 minutes. Add the onion and cook, stirring often, for 5 to 7 minutes, until softened and translucent.

2 Add the garlic, the whole hot peppers, and the chopped hot pepper and cook, stirring occasionally, for 1 to 2 minutes, until the garlic is fragrant. Add the chicken, along with the salt, turmeric, black pepper, and cayenne (if using). Cook, stirring occasionally, for 3 to 4 minutes, until the ingredients are well combined and the chicken is lightly golden. Stir in the tomato paste and cook for 1 minute.

3 Add 5 cups (1.2 L) of water and bring to a boil. Once boiling, cover the pot with the lid and let boil for 20 minutes over medium heat, stirring occasionally to prevent the onions from sticking to the bottom of the pot.

4 Remove the lid and stir the broth. Taste and adjust the salt; the broth should be noticeably salty. Add the pasta and 2 cups (480 ml) of water and stir well. Cover the pot again and reduce the heat to medium-low. Cook for 20 minutes, stirring every 5 minutes to ensure the pasta does not stick to the bottom of the pot, or until the pasta is cooked to desired doneness. Add more water as needed until the pasta is soft. Turn off the heat.

5 Garnish with the chopped parsley and serve immediately (the pasta should be moist when served).

Iraqi Kari Dejaj
CHICKEN CURRY

YIELD: 4 servings
PREP TIME: 10 minutes
COOK TIME: 40 minutes

◇◇◇◇◇

CHICKEN
1 teaspoon mild curry powder
½ teaspoon kosher salt
¼ teaspoon black pepper
1 tablespoon cornstarch
1 pound (454 g) boneless, skinless
   chicken thighs, cut into 1-inch
   (2.5 cm) cubes
2 tablespoons vegetable oil

CURRY
1 tablespoon vegetable oil
1 large yellow onion, finely chopped
1½ teaspoons kosher salt, divided
12 ounces (350 g) cremini
   mushrooms (or any other
   mushroom variety), sliced
2 large yellow potatoes, peeled and
   cut into 1-inch (2.5 cm) cubes
2½ teaspoons mild curry powder
¼ teaspoon black pepper
1 cup (135 g) frozen peas
3 cups (720 ml) chicken broth or
   water, divided
1 tablespoon cornstarch

FOR SERVING
Roz Bi Shaariya (page 67)

Note
To make this dish vegetarian,
skip the chicken and use
vegetable broth instead of
chicken broth. Follow the recipe
as directed starting with step 3.

Iraqis love using curry powder. It's made its way into many of our dishes, and we often rely on it to be the main seasoning blend. This kari is one example—a simple, quick, one-pan yellow curry made with chicken, potatoes, and peas and thickened with cornstarch. Using boneless chicken makes this recipe a fast one, but bone-in chicken will work wonderfully too, albeit with a slightly longer cook time. This dish is extremely comforting and excellent for weeknights. I love to make it extra saucy, with lots of potatoes, and serve it over a bowl of steaming Roz Bi Shaariya (page 67).

1 TO MAKE THE CHICKEN: In a large bowl, mix together the 1 teaspoon curry powder, ½ teaspoon salt, pepper, and cornstarch. Add the chicken cubes and thoroughly coat with the seasoning mix.

2 In a large skillet at least 2 inches (5 cm) deep, heat the 2 tablespoons vegetable oil over medium heat. Add the chicken cubes, working in batches if required, and sear for 1 to 2 minutes per side, until browned. Transfer to a plate.

3 TO MAKE THE CURRY: In the same skillet the chicken was cooked in, heat the 1 tablespoon vegetable oil over medium heat. Add the onion and ½ teaspoon of the salt and cook, stirring often, for 3 to 4 minutes, until the onion is softened. Add the mushrooms and continue to cook, stirring occasionally, for another 5 to 7 minutes, until browned.

4 Add the potatoes, 2½ teaspoons curry powder, pepper, and remaining 1 teaspoon salt. Mix well and cook for another 3 to 4 minutes. Add the peas and 2 cups (480 ml) of the broth. Bring to a simmer, then cover the skillet with a lid and let cook for 10 minutes.

5 Meanwhile, in a small bowl, mix the cornstarch with the remaining 1 cup (240 ml) broth and whisk until a smooth slurry forms.

6 After the 10 minutes, uncover the pan and add the slurry. Add the chicken back into the pan, mix well, and cook for another 15 to 20 minutes, uncovered, or until the chicken is cooked through and the vegetables are tender.

7 Serve with rice.

Sheet-Pan Honey Za'atar Chicken

YIELD: 4 servings
PREP TIME: 10 minutes
COOK TIME: 40 minutes

◇◇◇◇◇

VEGETABLES

3 large yellow potatoes (500 g), peeled and cut into ¼-inch (6 mm) wedges

1 large yellow onion, cut into eighths

7 small carrots (⅔ pound, or 300 g), sliced in half lengthwise and cut into 2-inch-long (5 cm) pieces

½ teaspoon kosher salt

1 tablespoon olive oil

CHICKEN

10 large cloves garlic, crushed into a paste using a small food processor, a mortar and pestle, or a garlic press

¼ cup (60 ml) olive oil

¼ cup (22 g) za'atar

2 teaspoons kosher salt

2 teaspoons onion powder

½ teaspoon black pepper

¼ cup (60 ml) honey

1 tablespoon apple cider vinegar

8 bone-in, skin-on chicken thighs (2⅔ pounds, or 1.2 kg), patted dry

FOR SERVING

Pita bread

Tahini Cabbage Slaw (page 48) or Arugula & Pomegranate Salad (page 52)

This was one of the first chicken dishes I created on my blog that went viral. And for good reason! It combines herby za'atar seasoning with honey and garlic to create a lip-smacking marinade that perfectly coats and flavors the chicken, carrots, and potatoes as they bake. This is the type of dish that doesn't quite make it to the table before I've had a full portion just for testing purposes. My favorite part is mopping up the juices in the bottom of the pan with a piece of pita bread.

1 Preheat the oven to 425°F (220°C). Line a large, rimmed sheet pan with parchment paper.

2 TO MAKE THE VEGETABLES: Add the potatoes, onion, and carrots to a large bowl. Season with the ½ teaspoon salt, drizzle with the 1 tablespoon oil, and mix all the ingredients together. Transfer to the prepared sheet pan and spread in a single layer.

3 TO MAKE THE CHICKEN: In a small bowl, combine the garlic, ¼ cup (60 ml) oil, za'atar, 2 teaspoons salt, onion powder, pepper, honey, and vinegar and mix well.

4 Place the chicken thighs on the sheet pan with the vegetables. Pour all the marinade over the chicken and work it into each piece, ensuring both the fronts and backs of the thighs are coated. Work a few tablespoons of the marinade into the vegetables as well.

5 Bake for 35 to 40 minutes, until the thighs are golden brown and cooked through. (Check that the chicken is white on the inside and the juices run clear.)

6 Spoon the vegetables onto a platter and top with the chicken. Serve with pita bread and slaw or salad.

Persian Fesenjoon
POMEGRANATE & WALNUT CHICKEN STEW

YIELD: 4 servings

PREP TIME: 10 minutes

COOK TIME: 45 minutes

◇◇◇◇◇

1½ pounds (650 g) bone-in, skin-on chicken thighs (4 or 5 thighs)

2 teaspoons kosher salt, divided

¼ teaspoon black pepper

¼ teaspoon ground turmeric

2 tablespoons olive oil

1 large onion, finely chopped

2 cups (200 g) unsalted whole raw walnuts

½ cup (120 ml) pomegranate molasses

½ teaspoon granulated sugar

FOR GARNISHING AND SERVING

½ cup (96 g) pomegranate arils

2 tablespoons finely chopped fresh parsley

Roz Bi Shaariya (page 67) or Roz Asfar (page 71)

A love for sweet-and-sour stews goes back to ancient times, when that flavor profile came to Middle Eastern cuisine. Pomegranate juice was one of the most common ways that tartness was infused into savory dishes, and this Persian fesenjoon is one of the most popular dishes that heavily uses pomegranate. It's made in modern-day Iran as well as in the central and southern cities of Iraq. You can use red meat or chicken, in which the bone-in meat is simmered with onions and turmeric and then thickened with pulverized walnuts and flavored with a generous amount of pomegranate molasses. It is important to also add a bit of sugar to balance the tartness. The result is a thick, brown stew, and while not the most appealing in looks, it has an incredible amount of umami and depth for a stew that comes together surprisingly quick.

1 In a large bowl or plate, evenly sprinkle the chicken thighs with ½ teaspoon of the salt, the pepper, and turmeric.

2 In a large pot, heat the oil over medium heat. Add the chicken thighs, skin sides down, and sear them for 1 to 2 minutes per side. Add the onion and cook, stirring often, until softened, 5 to 6 minutes. Cover the chicken and onion with water and add 1 teaspoon of the salt. Bring to a boil, then cover with the lid and let boil over medium-low heat for 30 minutes.

3 Meanwhile, pulse the walnuts in a food processor until a fine consistency, like a fine flour.

4 Add the ground walnuts to a large, dry skillet and toast over low heat for 5 minutes, or until fragrant, stirring continuously. (To ensure the walnuts do not burn, remove from the heat as soon as they are fragrant.) Add the toasted walnuts to the pot, cover the pot halfway with the lid, and continue to simmer for 15 minutes, adding more water if required to ensure the chicken is mostly submerged and the stew consistency is not too thick. Stir occasionally.

5 Add the pomegranate molasses and sugar. Stir, taste, and adjust the seasoning by adding the remaining ½ teaspoon salt if necessary. Let simmer for 10 to 15 minutes, uncovered, then turn off the heat. The stew consistency should be thick but pourable; the texture will be slightly grainy, which is fine.

6 Garnish with the pomegranate arils and chopped parsley and serve with rice.

Weeknight Iraqi Chicken Biryani

YIELD: 6 servings
PREP TIME: 15 minutes
COOK TIME: 50 minutes

◇◇◇◇◇

POTATOES

3 large yellow potatoes (about
   1½ pounds, or 650 g), peeled and
   cut into ¾-inch (2 cm) cubes
2 tablespoons avocado oil
½ teaspoon salt

CHICKEN

1½ pounds (700 g) boneless, skinless
   chicken thighs, cut into ¾-inch
   (2 cm) cubes (see Note on
   page 124)
1½ teaspoons kosher salt
¼ teaspoon black pepper
¼ teaspoon ground cardamom
¼ teaspoon ground cinnamon
¼ teaspoon ground cloves
1 tablespoon avocado oil

RICE

3 tablespoons avocado oil
1½ teaspoons salt
½ teaspoon ground turmeric
2 cups (400 g) long-grain white
   basmati rice, rinsed until the water
   runs clear and drained completely
1½ cups (200 g) frozen green peas

You may be surprised to see a biryani recipe in a Middle Eastern cookbook, given its prominence in South Asian cuisine. However, food travels widely, and it is believed that biryani actually originated in Persia and eventually made its way to India, where it was adapted to local cooking techniques and flavors. Nowadays, biryani is common across Arabic countries, most notably in Iraq and the Persian Gulf. It is quite different from South Asian biryani, using other spices and cooking techniques. This recipe is unique to my family's region of Iraq and is how my mom made it when I was growing up, usually with chicken and flavored heavily with her mix of baharat (seasoning). The spices are added at the end without cooking, which is a unique technique that allows the flavor of every spice to shine through. This recipe made my mom's dinner table quite popular with friends and family, and it was often requested. I have streamlined the process, using the oven as well as the stove, and skipping the longer step of poaching chicken, in the hopes that it can be a dish you will happily make and enjoy on a weeknight. This dish is such a treat, with so much texture and bursts of flavors all in one bite.

1 TO MAKE THE POTATOES: Preheat the oven to 450°F (230°C) and position a rack on the bottom. Line a large baking sheet with parchment paper.

2 Add the potatoes to the sheet pan and toss with the 2 tablespoons oil and ½ teaspoon salt. Smooth the cubes into a single layer and bake for 25 to 30 minutes on the bottom rack, until golden and soft.

3 MEANWHILE, MAKE THE CHICKEN: Add the chicken to a large bowl with the 1½ teaspoons salt and ¼ teaspoon each of pepper, cardamom, cinnamon, and cloves. Mix well to thoroughly coat the chicken.

4 In a large, deep skillet, heat the 1 tablespoon oil over medium heat. Add the chicken and cook, working in batches to avoid overcrowding, for a few minutes, until seared on both sides; it does not need to cook through. Transfer to a plate.

CONTINUED ▶

BAHARAT SPICE BLEND

1 teaspoon black pepper
1 teaspoon curry powder
1 teaspoon ground allspice
1 teaspoon ground cinnamon
1 teaspoon ground cardamom
½ teaspoon ground nutmeg
½ teaspoon ground cumin
½ teaspoon ground cloves

FOR GARNISHING AND SERVING

1 tablespoon avocado oil
½ cup (55 g) slivered almonds
1 cup (145 g) raisins (optional)
Plain, whole-milk yogurt
Salata (page 44)

5 TO MAKE THE RICE: In the same skillet the chicken was cooked in, heat the 3 tablespoons oil over medium heat. Add the 1½ teaspoons salt and the turmeric, mix, and then add the rice and 3 cups (720 ml) of water. Bring to a boil. Once boiling, add the chicken back into the skillet over the rice and sprinkle the frozen peas on top. Cover the skillet with a tight-fitting lid, reduce the heat to low, and let cook for 20 minutes, undisturbed.

6 MEANWHILE, MAKE THE BAHARAT SPICE BLEND: In a small bowl, mix together all the spice blend ingredients.

7 TO MAKE THE GARNISH: In a small skillet, heat the 1 tablespoon oil over low heat, then add the almonds and toast for 2 to 3 minutes until golden, stirring continuously. Transfer to a small bowl. Add the raisins (if using) to the skillet and heat them through, about 30 seconds.

8 After the biryani has cooked for 20 minutes, remove the lid and gently fluff the rice with a fork or wooden spoon. Sprinkle the baharat spice blend all over the rice and mix gently. Cover and let the rice steam for 10 more minutes with the heat off.

9 Spoon the biryani into a large serving tray and add the potatoes on top along with half of the toasted almonds and raisins (if using). Stir gently until everything is combined.

10 Garnish with the remaining toasted almonds and raisins (if using) and serve with yogurt and salad.

Note

The chicken in this recipe can be swapped for small beef meatballs. Use the meatballs recipe in Shorbat Lsan El Asfoor (page 205). Cook the meatballs the same way as the chicken.

Sheet-Pan Palestinian Musakhan

SUMAC-ROASTED CHICKEN & ONIONS

YIELD: 4 to 6 servings
PREP TIME: 10 minutes
COOK TIME: 50 minutes

◇◇◇◇◇

ONIONS

3 large red onions (1¾ pounds, or 800 g), cut in half, then thinly sliced into half-moons (use a sharp knife, mandoline, or food processor with a slicer attachment)

2 tablespoons sumac

1 teaspoon kosher salt

¼ cup (60 ml) olive oil

CHICKEN

2 teaspoons kosher salt

1 teaspoon black pepper

2½ teaspoons seven spice

1 teaspoon ground cumin

3 tablespoons sumac

2 tablespoons olive oil

Juice of 1 large lemon

6 bone-in, skin-on chicken leg quarters (4½ to 5½ pounds, or 2 to 2.5 kg), excess fat trimmed

Palestine is known for its high-quality olive oil, and musakhan is a dish that is centered around celebrating this ingredient. It is known to be Palestine's national dish and consists of heavily seasoned, roasted chicken served atop layers of taboon bread smothered in sumac and onions that have been slowly caramelized in plenty of olive oil. It is traditionally served family-style on a large platter, with guests using their hands to rip off pieces of chicken and roll it up in the soft bread. The tartness of the sumac and sweetness of the onions are a perfect combination. The authentic way of making this dish requires slowly caramelizing the onions in a large pan with lots of olive oil. In this more streamlined version of musakhan, I roast the onions and chicken together on one sheet pan with enough olive oil to keep them moist. This method works really well and transforms the dish into a weeknight staple.

1 Preheat the oven to 400°F (205°C) and place a rack in the middle.

2 TO MAKE THE ONIONS: Line a large, rimmed sheet pan with parchment paper. Add the onions to the middle of the sheet pan with the 2 tablespoons sumac, 1 teaspoon salt, and ¼ cup (60 ml) oil. Mix well to thoroughly coat the onions. Spread the onions in a single layer, covering the pan's full surface area.

3 TO MAKE THE CHICKEN: In a small bowl, mix together the 2 teaspoons salt, pepper, seven spice, cumin, and 3 tablespoons sumac with the 2 tablespoons oil and the lemon juice to create a thick paste.

4 Evenly slather the spice paste all over the chicken, gently massaging it into each leg and working the paste under the skin as well. Place the chicken on the sheet pan on top of the onions.

5 Place the sheet pan in the oven on the middle rack and bake the chicken for 45 to 50 minutes, until cooked through. (Check that the chicken is white on the inside and the juices run clear.) The onions at the edges of the pan will start to caramelize; this is normal and will add a lot of flavor. Broil the chicken for 3 to 4 minutes until golden brown.

CONTINUED ▶

FOR GARNISHING AND SERVING

2 teaspoons olive oil

¼ cup pine nuts (35 g) or slivered
    almonds (30 g)

2 large taboon or lavash bread
    (14 inches, or 35 cm; see Note
    (or substitute 6 of any other
    8-inch, or 20-cm, flatbread)

2 tablespoons sumac

¼ cup (13 g) finely chopped fresh
    parsley

Plain, whole-milk yogurt

Salata (page 44) or Arugula &
    Pomegranate Salad (page 52)

6 TO MAKE THE GARNISH: In a small skillet, heat the olive oil over low heat, then add the pine nuts and toast for 2 to 3 minutes, until golden, stirring continuously.

7 Remove the chicken from the sheet pan. Take one of the pieces of taboon bread and smear it in the chicken juices in the sheet pan to soak up some of the liquid, then place it on a large platter, juicy side up. Scoop half of the onions from the sheet pan and spread them on the bread in a thin layer. Repeat with the remaining piece of bread, placing it on another platter and adding the remaining onions on top. Place 3 chicken quarters on top of each piece of bread.

8 Garnish with a dusting of the 2 tablespoons sumac and sprinkle the toasted almonds and chopped parsley over everything. Serve each person a piece of chicken with some bread and onions along with yogurt and salad.

Note

If you are serving fewer people, you may use only 1 large taboon bread and serve the rest of the bread on the side for easier leftovers storage.

One-Pot Harissa Chicken & Rice

YIELD: 6 servings
PREP TIME: 15 minutes
COOK TIME: 45 minutes

◇◇◇◇◇

6 skin-on, bone-in chicken thighs
    (2¼ pounds, or 1 kg)
3¾ teaspoons kosher salt, divided,
    plus more if needed
¼ cup (95 g) Tunisian Harissa
    (page 25)
3 tablespoons Toum (page 22)
    (or substitute 6 large cloves
    garlic, crushed)
Juice of ½ lemon
3 tablespoons olive oil
1 small onion, finely chopped
3 cups (90 g) packed chopped
    spinach
18 ounces (510 g) chickpeas, drained
    and rinsed
2 cups (400 g) long-grain white
    basmati rice, rinsed until the water
    runs clear and drained completely
4 cups (960 ml) chicken broth
    or water

FOR SERVING
Fresh lemon juice
Salata (page 44), Tahini Cabbage
    Slaw (page 48), or Arugula &
    Pomegranate Salad (page 52)
Plain, whole-milk yogurt

Note
Store-bought and homemade
chicken broths have different
salt content, so taste, then
adjust the salt as necessary.

I cook a lot of chicken and rice at my home, and this is one of the ways I like to change it up using two condiments I typically have on hand: Tunisian Harissa (page 25) and Toum (page 22). Skin-on, bone-in chicken thighs are marinated and then seared until golden. The rice is cooked in the same pot, along with chickpeas and spinach to bulk it up. The thighs then go back on top and the whole thing steams for twenty minutes before you're ready to serve it. It's a quick, weeknight-friendly favorite.

1 In a large bowl, season the chicken thighs with 1¼ teaspoons of the salt on both sides. Add the harissa, toum, and lemon juice and mix well to thoroughly coat the chicken. You can cover and let the chicken marinate for 1 to 2 hours in the refrigerator for optimal flavor, or use it right away.

2 In a large, 2-inch (5 cm) deep skillet with a tight-fitting lid, heat the oil over medium heat. Add the chicken thighs, reserving any marinade, and sear them, skin sides down, for 2 to 3 minutes, until golden brown. Flip and sear on the other side for 2 to 3 minutes. Work in batches to avoid overcrowding if necessary, transferring the chicken to a plate. If there are any burnt seasonings in the skillet, remove them with a spoon but keep the oil.

3 In the same skillet over medium heat, add the onion along with any reserved chicken marinade and cook, stirring often, until softened and translucent, 6 to 7 minutes.

4 Add the spinach, chickpeas, and 1 teaspoon of the salt. Cook and stir until the spinach wilts, 2 to 3 minutes.

5 Add the rice and stir to combine with the chickpeas and vegetables. Add the chicken broth and the remaining 1½ teaspoons salt. Bring to a boil over medium heat. Once boiling, carefully taste and adjust the salt if necessary; it should taste noticeably salty (see Note).

6 Add the chicken thighs back into the pan, arranging them on top of the rice. Cover the pot, reduce the heat to low, and let cook, undisturbed, for 25 minutes. Remove the lid and fluff the rice using a fork.

7 Serve warm with slaw or salad and yogurt.

Apricot Chicken

YIELD: 4 to 6 servings

PREP TIME: 10 minutes

COOK TIME: 45 minutes

◇◇◇◇◇

CHICKEN

6 bone-in, skin-on, chicken thighs
(1⅔ pounds, or 750 g)

1 teaspoon kosher salt

½ teaspoon black pepper

1 tablespoon olive oil

SAUCE

1 large onion, thinly sliced

1 teaspoon kosher salt

2 cups (350 g) dried apricots, cut
into quarters

½ teaspoon ground cardamom

½ teaspoon ground cumin

½ teaspoon ground coriander

2 tablespoons granulated sugar

FOR GARNISHING AND SERVING

2 tablespoons chopped pistachios

1 tablespoon slivered almonds

1 tablespoon unsalted chopped
raw walnuts

Roz Bi Shaariya (page 67)

This dish is a nod to an ancient Iraqi dish called *torshana* or *qaysi*, which is a sweet-and-sour stew made of apricots, prunes, and lamb. The stew is thick and jammy in consistency and served over rice. Growing up, I never really liked it because I always found it to be too sweet. But I am definitely in the minority; most Iraqis love this dish. I do, however, love the idea of using sweet and tangy apricots in savory applications, and given that chicken is a much quicker protein to cook than lamb, I developed this recipe. This dish is different and truly delicious.

1 Preheat the oven to 400°F (205°C) and place a rack in the middle.

2 TO MAKE THE CHICKEN: Season the chicken thighs on both sides with the salt and pepper.

3 In a 12-inch (30 cm) oven-safe skillet (preferably cast iron), heat the oil over medium-high heat. Add the chicken thighs and sear them, skin sides down, for 1 to 2 minutes, until golden. Flip and sear the other side for another few minutes. Work in batches to avoid overcrowding. Transfer to a plate.

4 TO MAKE THE SAUCE: In the same skillet, add the onion and the salt. Reduce the heat to medium and cook, stirring often, for 4 to 5 minutes, until the onion is softened and golden. Add the apricots and cook for 1 to 2 minutes. Add the cardamom, cumin, and coriander and mix to combine. Cook for 1 to 2 minutes longer.

5 Add the sugar and 3 cups (720 ml) of water and bring to a boil over medium heat. Let boil for 5 to 7 minutes, until slightly reduced. Add the chicken thighs back into the skillet, skin sides up.

6 Place the skillet in the oven, uncovered, and bake for 30 to 40 minutes, until the chicken is fully cooked (white on the inside or has an internal temperature of 165°F, or 74°C). Keep a close eye on the water level, adding more as needed to avoid the sauce drying up; the sauce should be a thick consistency. Remove from the oven and let rest for 10 minutes.

7 MEANWHILE, MAKE THE GARNISH: Toast the nuts in a small, dry skillet over low heat for a few minutes, or until fragrant, stirring continuously.

8 Garnish the chicken with the toasted nuts and serve with rice.

Roasted Baharat Chicken & Potatoes

YIELD: 4 to 6 servings

PREP TIME: 10 minutes

COOK TIME: 1 hour

◇◇◇◇◇

7 large cloves garlic, minced

½ teaspoon black pepper

½ teaspoon curry powder

½ teaspoon ground allspice

½ teaspoon ground cinnamon

½ teaspoon ground cardamom

¼ teaspoon ground nutmeg

¼ teaspoon ground cumin

¼ teaspoon ground cloves

2 teaspoons kosher salt, divided

¼ cup (60 ml) olive oil

1 tablespoon apple cider vinegar

8 boneless, skinless chicken thighs
(1½ pounds, or 665 g)

4 large yellow potatoes, cut into
thick wedges

1 large red onion, cut into thick
wedges

FOR GARNISHING AND SERVING

¼ cup (13 g) finely chopped fresh
parsley

¼ cup (15 g) finely chopped green
onions

Arugula & Pomegranate Salad
(page 52) or Tahini Cabbage Slaw
(page 48)

There's no dish more universal than chicken and potatoes. I make some version of it on a weekly basis, with eyeballed measurements and throwing in what I have on hand. This recipe was made using my mom's baharat spice blend from her famous Chicken Biryani (page 122). This is an easy, hands-off meal that is bursting with flavor. Don't forget to mop up the juices with a piece of bread.

1 Preheat the oven to 450°F (230°C) and place a rack in the middle.

2 In a large bowl, mix together the garlic, pepper, curry powder, allspice, cinnamon, cardamom, nutmeg, cumin, cloves, 1 teaspoon of the salt, oil, and the vinegar to create a thick paste. Remove 3 tablespoons of the paste and set aside.

3 Add the chicken thighs to the bowl and mix with the marinade until the chicken is thoroughly coated. Let marinate for 30 minutes.

4 Meanwhile, place the potato and onion wedges in a large baking dish (at least 13 x 11 inches, or 33 x 28 cm). Add the remaining 1 teaspoon salt and reserved marinade and mix well to combine; arrange the potatoes and onions in a single layer.

5 Place the baking dish in the oven and bake for 15 minutes, uncovered. Remove the dish from the oven. Nestle the marinated chicken thighs on top of the potatoes and onions, add ¾ cup (180 ml) of water, and return the dish to the oven and bake, uncovered, for another 30 minutes. Test the chicken and potatoes for doneness. The potatoes should be soft and the chicken white on the inside or cooked to 165°F (74°C). Baste the chicken with the juices from the bottom of the pan, then broil for 3 to 5 minutes, until lightly golden on top.

6 Garnish the dish with the chopped parsley and green onions and serve with salad or slaw.

One-Pot Chicken & Mushroom Bulgur

YIELD: 6 servings
PREP TIME: 10 minutes
COOK TIME: 50 minutes

◇◇◇◇◇

1½ pounds (680 g) boneless, skinless chicken thighs, cut into ½-inch (13 mm) cubes

3 teaspoons kosher salt, divided, plus more to taste

1 teaspoon black pepper, divided

2 teaspoons ground cumin, divided

1½ teaspoons ground coriander, divided

4 tablespoons olive oil, divided

1½ pounds (680 g) cremini mushrooms, thinly sliced

3 small yellow onions, finely diced

½ teaspoon ground turmeric

18 ounces (510 g) chickpeas, rinsed and drained

2 cups (410 g) coarse bulgur, rinsed and drained

3 cups (720 ml) chicken broth

FOR SERVING

Salata (page 44) or Arugula & Pomegranate Salad (page 52)

Plain, whole-milk yogurt

This bulgur dish is cooked Iraqi-style, with lots of mushrooms, onions, and boneless chicken pieces. The combination of those ingredients adds so much umami to this dish that I can't help but eat spoon after spoon standing at the stove. It's important to cook the mushrooms down on their own, without much oil, and give them time to release their moisture and turn golden brown; that's how their flavor will concentrate. I serve this dish with any citrusy side salad and dollops of plain yogurt.

1 Add the chicken pieces to a medium bowl and sprinkle with 2 teaspoons of the salt, ½ teaspoon of the pepper, 1 teaspoon of the cumin, and 1 teaspoon of the coriander. Mix to combine well.

2 In a large, 2-inch (5 cm) deep skillet or medium pot, heat 1 tablespoon of the oil over medium heat. Add the chicken and, working in batches to avoid overcrowding, sear the chicken pieces for 2 minutes per side, or until golden. Transfer to a plate.

3 Add the mushrooms to the same skillet and cook, stirring often, over medium heat for 10 minutes, until they turn deeply golden and release their moisture. Add the onions and remaining 3 tablespoons oil and cook until softened, stirring often, for 5 to 6 minutes. Add the remaining 1 teaspoon salt, ½ teaspoon pepper, 1 teaspoon cumin, and ½ teaspoon coriander along with the turmeric and stir to combine. Mix to combine and toast the spices for 2 minutes, or until fragrant. Remove a few tablespoons of the onion and mushroom mixture for garnish, if desired.

4 Add the chickpeas, bulgur, and broth and bring to a boil. Once boiling, carefully taste the liquid and adjust the salt; it should be noticeably salty. Add the chicken back into the skillet, cover with the lid, reduce the heat to low, and let cook for 25 minutes, undisturbed. Remove the lid and fluff the bulgur with a fork.

5 Garnish with the reserved mushrooms and onions (if using) and serve with salad and yogurt.

Note

To make this dish vegetarian, skip the chicken and follow the recipe as directed starting with step 3.

Egyptian Macarona Bechamel
BAKED PASTA CASSEROLE

YIELD: 6 servings
PREP TIME: 10 minutes
COOK TIME: 50 minutes

◇◇◇◇◇

BEEF SAUCE AND PASTA

1 tablespoon olive oil
1 medium yellow onion, finely chopped
1½ pounds (680 g) lean ground beef
3 teaspoons kosher salt, divided
3 teaspoons ground allspice
1 teaspoon ground cinnamon
1 teaspoon black pepper
1 teaspoon onion powder
1 teaspoon garlic powder
2½ cups (360 ml) tomato passata (puree)
16 ounces (454 g) penne pasta
4 cups (960 ml) boiling water

BECHAMEL SAUCE

¾ cup (180 g) unsalted butter
¾ cup (100 g) all-purpose flour
3 cups plus 2 tablespoons (750 ml) whole milk
1½ teaspoons kosher salt
½ teaspoon black pepper
½ teaspoon ground nutmeg

This is a decadent pasta dish that is a constant go-to for dinner parties. It's traditionally made in three layers: a layer of al dente pasta coated in a luscious, smooth, and buttery bechamel sauce; a layer of a meat-based ragù seasoned with warm spices; and a thick layer of bechamel. The layers are then baked until their flavors infuse together. My favorite thing about it is how it looks when the top is broiled and beautiful brown spots form. This dish is a result of the diversity in Egypt before the twentieth century. Think of it as a cross between the Greek pastitsio and Italian lasagna, using the classic recipe for French bechamel. And, of course, every Egyptian mother and grandmother adds her own special touch.

1 Preheat the oven to 400°F (205°C).

2 TO MAKE THE BEEF SAUCE AND PASTA: In a large, 2-inch (5 cm) deep, oven-safe skillet, heat the oil over medium heat. Add the onion and cook, stirring often, until softened, 5 minutes. Add the ground beef and cook, breaking it up into small pieces with a wooden spoon, for 5 to 7 minutes, until browned and the liquid has released. Add 2½ teaspoons of the salt, the allspice, cinnamon, 1 teaspoon pepper, onion powder, garlic powder, and passata and cook for 5 to 7 more minutes.

3 Add the uncooked pasta to the pan along with the boiling water and the remaining ½ teaspoon salt. Stir to combine, cover with the lid, and cook for 15 minutes, stirring every 5 minutes or so to prevent the pasta from sticking to the skillet. If the pasta still has a bit of a bite, that is fine as it will continue cooking in the oven. Turn the heat off.

4 MEANWHILE, MAKE THE BECHAMEL SAUCE: In a medium saucepan, melt the butter over medium-low heat. Add the flour and whisk vigorously for 4 to 5 minutes, until the flour absorbs all the butter and looks dry. Add the milk gradually and continue whisking the bechamel for 8 to 10 minutes, until it starts to thicken. Stir in the 1½ teaspoons salt, ½ teaspoon pepper, and nutmeg. Dip a spoon into the bechamel, then run your finger down the spoon's back; if the sauce separates, it is ready.

5 Mix the pasta and beef sauce one more time and use a spoon to flatten its surface. Slowly pour the bechamel on top, spreading it evenly.

6 Bake, uncovered, for 20 to 25 minutes. If the sauce starts to leak to the top and around the edges, that's normal. Broil the top for 3 to 4 minutes, until golden, then serve immediately.

Syrian Kousa Bi Laban

UNSTUFFED ZUCCHINI IN YOGURT

YIELD: 4 servings
PREP TIME: 15 minutes
COOK TIME: 45 minutes

◇◇◇◇◇

ZUCCHINI

3 large zucchini (about 1½ pounds, or 660 g, total)
1 tablespoon olive oil
¾ teaspoon kosher salt

GROUND BEEF

2 tablespoons olive oil
1 large yellow onion, finely chopped
1 teaspoon kosher salt, divided, plus more if needed
1 pound (454 g) lean ground beef
1 teaspoon seven spice
¼ teaspoon black pepper
½ cup (70 g) pine nuts (or substitute slivered almonds)

YOGURT SAUCE

4½ cups (1.1 L) plain, whole-milk yogurt
1 tablespoon cornstarch
1 large egg
1 teaspoon kosher salt
1 teaspoon dried mint

FOR GARNISHING AND SERVING

Dried mint
Roz Bi Shaariya (page 67)

Note

You can serve this dish layered in a deep serving platter. Layer the beef, zucchini, and yogurt, then garnish with pine nuts and dried mint.

Kousa means "squash" or "zucchini" in Arabic, and it is one of the vegetables that is most commonly cored and stuffed with ground beef. The stuffed kousa are then either simmered in a rich tomato sauce or a yogurt sauce. I personally always gravitate to warm, cooked yogurt dishes, and this is one of my favorites. But instead of going through the process of coring and stuffing the zucchini, which can be very time-consuming, I make a deconstructed version on the advice of my Syrian friend Nadia (who is an excellent cook).

1 TO MAKE THE ZUCCHINI: Preheat the oven to 400°F (205°C). Line a large, rimmed sheet pan with parchment paper.

2 Cut the zucchini in half lengthwise, then cut in half lengthwise again. Each zucchini will create 4 long "sticks." Finally, cut the 12 sticks into ½-inch-long (13 mm) pieces. Place the pieces on the prepared sheet pan. Drizzle with the 1 tablespoon oil and sprinkle with the ¾ teaspoon salt, toss to combine. Bake for 20 to 30 minutes, until soft; if required, bake for another 5 to 10 minutes.

3 TO MAKE THE GROUND BEEF: In a large skillet, heat the 2 tablespoons oil over medium heat. Add the onion and ½ teaspoon of the salt and cook, stirring often, until softened, 5 to 6 minutes. Add the ground beef and cook, breaking it up into small pieces with a wooden spoon, for 6 to 7 minutes, until browned and its juices dry up. Season with the remaining ½ teaspoon salt, seven spice, and pepper and cook and stir for a few minutes longer to combine the spices with the beef. Taste and adjust the salt if necessary. Using the wooden spoon, move the beef to one side of the skillet and add the pine nuts to the other side. Toast them for a few minutes, or until lightly golden. Remove a few tablespoons of pine nuts and set aside for garnishing, then mix the rest with the meat. Turn off the heat.

4 TO MAKE THE YOGURT SAUCE: Add the yogurt to a medium saucepan but do not turn on the heat. Place the cornstarch in a small bowl with 3 tablespoons of water. Whisk together with a fork to create a slurry. Add the slurry to the yogurt along with the egg. Whisk well to combine, then turn the heat to medium. Let the yogurt heat up and simmer for 10 to 12 minutes, whisking occasionally. Do not bring it to a boil. Season with the 1 teaspoon salt and mint and turn off the heat. Add the baked zucchini and ground beef and gently mix to combine. Garnish with the reserved pine nuts and mint. Serve with rice.

One-Pot Hashweh Rice

YIELD: 4 to 6 servings
PREP TIME: 10 minutes
COOK TIME: 40 minutes

◇◇◇◇◇

3 tablespoons vegetable oil
1 large yellow onion, finely chopped
1 pound (454 g) lean ground beef
2½ teaspoons ground allspice
1 teaspoon ground cinnamon
2½ teaspoons kosher salt, divided
½ teaspoon black pepper
2 cups (270 g) frozen peas (or a mix
   of peas and carrots)
2 cups (400 g) long-grain white
   basmati rice, rinsed until the water
   runs clear and drained completely

FOR GARNISHING AND SERVING
1 tablespoon vegetable oil
½ cup (55 g) slivered almonds
   (optional)
¼ cup (35 g) raisins (optional)
¼ cup (13 g) fresh parsley leaves
Plain, whole-milk yogurt
Salata (page 44)

Back in my dark, blurry days, which was when I was working a full-time engineering job, commuting to the office every day, and juggling two little kids at home, I'd get home and rush to the kitchen, still in my work clothes, and quickly make this recipe. It was a go-to meal because it had protein, carbs, and vegetables all in one pot and required very easy sides: a bowl of plain yogurt and maybe a quick chopped salad, if I could swing it. This dish is called *hashweh* rice, which translates to "filling," because the seasoned ground beef is used as a filling, in many traditional dishes. If my mom had leftover hashweh, she would always turn it into this rice dish with peas and carrots.

1 In a large pot, heat the 3 tablespoons oil over medium heat. Add the onion and cook, stirring often, until softened, about 5 minutes.

2 Add the ground beef and cook, breaking it up into small pieces with a wooden spoon, for 7 to 10 minutes, until browned and the juices start to dry up.

3 Add the allspice, cinnamon, 1 teaspoon of the salt, the pepper, and peas. Stir to combine and continue to cook for 5 to 7 minutes, until the mixture looks dry and not much moisture is left.

4 Add the rice to the pot along with 3 cups (720 ml) of water and the remaining 1½ teaspoons salt. Mix well to combine and ensure the water completely covers the rice mixture. Increase the heat to medium-high and let the mixture come to a boil; this should take only a few minutes. As soon as it starts boiling, cover immediately with the lid and reduce the heat to low. Let cook for 20 minutes, undisturbed.

5 MEANWHILE, IF USING THE ALMONDS AND/OR RAISINS, MAKE THE GARNISH: Heat the 1 tablespoon oil in a small skillet over medium-low heat, then add the almonds and toast them for 4 to 5 minutes, until golden brown, stirring continuously. Transfer to a small bowl. Add the raisins to the skillet and warm them through, about 30 seconds.

6 After the rice has cooked for 20 minutes, turn off the heat and let the pot sit, covered, for 10 minutes more. Remove the lid and fluff the rice with a fork or wooden spoon,

7 Spoon into a serving dish and garnish with the almonds (if using), raisins (if using), and parsley. Serve with yogurt and salad.

Lebanese Arayes
STUFFED PITA

YIELD: 8 pieces

PREP TIME: 15 minutes

COOK TIME: 30 minutes

◇◇◇◇◇

½ large yellow onion, roughly chopped

5 large cloves garlic, peeled

½ cup (25 g) packed roughly chopped fresh parsley

1 pound (454 g) extra-lean ground beef

4 tablespoons olive oil, divided, plus more for greasing

½ teaspoon black pepper

1 teaspoon kosher salt

1 teaspoon seven spice (or substitute with ground allspice)

2 tablespoons pomegranate molasses

4 small, thick Greek-style round pitas (4 inches, or 10 cm), cut in half (see Note)

FOR SERVING

Tarator (page 30), Toum (page 22), and/or ketchup

French fries

Note

To bake, preheat the oven to 400°F (205°C). Place a wire rack on top of a large, rimmed sheet pan and arrange the arayes on the rack, side by side. Bake for 20 minutes, flipping them halfway through, then broil for a few minutes until crisp.

To this day, I'm still not sure why this dish is called *arayes*, which literally translates to "brides" in Arabic. But no matter, it will continue to be a constant go-to meal for my family, because it uses one of my favorite versatile proteins to cook with in a fun way. Arayes are usually made at barbecues using raw kofta smeared inside pita bread, which is crisped up on the grill until the beef is juicy and cooked through. They're a popular Levantine street food but also a perfect weeknight dinner that guarantees happy bellies (especially little ones). No need to fire up the grill; these come out perfectly crispy and delicious when grilled on a stovetop cast-iron pan or baked in the oven.

1 Add the onion, garlic, and parsley to a small food processor and pulse until chopped very fine. (If you do not have a food processor, you can chop it very finely with a knife.) Using your hands, squeeze out and discard as much moisture as you can from this vegetable mixture and transfer it to a large bowl.

2 Add the ground beef, 2 tablespoons of the oil, the pepper, salt, seven spice, and pomegranate molasses. Mix well using your hands, ensuring all the spices are well incorporated.

3 Open the pita halves to form pockets. Stuff each one with about 2 tablespoons of the meat mixture, ensuring the meat layer is roughly ¼ to ½ inch (6 to 13 mm) thick. Press down to flatten and ensure the filling comes all the way to the edge.

4 Brush the outsides of the pitas with the remaining 2 or 3 tablespoons oil on all sides.

5 Preheat a medium or large cast-iron grill pan over high heat. Brush with olive oil, then place 2 or 3 pitas (however many you can fit) in the pan and sear for 2 minutes per side, pressing down lightly with a spatula. Sear the edges as well, especially the exposed meat side. Continue to cook, flipping the arayes every 1 to 2 minutes, until the beef is cooked through and the outside is golden, 5 to 7 minutes total. Repeat with the remaining pitas.

6 Serve immediately with tarator, toum, and/or ketchup for dipping and french fries.

Sheet-Pan Iraqi Aroog
BEEF PATTIES

YIELD: 25 to 30 pieces; 4 to 6 servings

PREP TIME: 15 minutes

COOK TIME: 40 minutes

◇◇◇◇◇

2 medium yellow onions, peeled and roughly chopped

1 small bunch fresh parsley, roughly chopped

2 large cloves garlic, peeled

1 small bell pepper (any color), roughly chopped

1¾ pounds (800 g) regular or lean ground beef

2 teaspoons kosher salt

1 teaspoon black pepper

1¼ cups (155 g) all-purpose flour

1 cup (240 ml) tomato passata (puree)

¼ cup tomato paste

½ teaspoon baking powder

4 tablespoons vegetable oil

FOR SERVING

Fresh samoon buns or pita bread

Sliced tomatoes

Sliced green onions

Roughly chopped fresh parsley

Mayonnaise, hot sauce, and/or ketchup

Note

You may also shallow-fry these beef patties in a nonstick skillet using roughly ½ inch (13 mm) of oil, working in batches.

Aroog are an Iraqi pan-fried beef patty made with onions, garlic, parsley, and sometimes peppers or tomatoes. They are lightly seasoned and flavored mostly with tomato sauce. These crispy patties are often served as a light dinner or stuffed into Iraqi *samoon* (buns) with sliced veggies. My sisters and I would request aroog often, and we'd stand around my mom in the kitchen as she pan-fried them, with oil splattering all over the stove. As soon as she'd place the first few pieces on the plate, we would immediately dive in, rolling them up in bread, always with slices of tomato, parsley, and onions. And because the oil splattering is such a vivid memory, and I do not enjoy cleaning my stove, I came up with a sheet-pan version that mimics the pan frying in a cleaner, faster way, along with being great for making large batches.

1 Preheat the oven to 450°F (230°C) and position a rack on the bottom.

2 Add the onions, parsley, garlic, and bell pepper to a food processor and pulse until chopped very fine. (If you do not have a food processor, you can chop very finely with a knife.)

3 Transfer the mixture to a large bowl, then add the ground beef, salt, pepper, flour, passata, tomato paste, and baking powder. Mix well with your hands until the mixture is cohesive and forms a soft dough.

4 Line two large, rimmed sheet pans with parchment paper, then pour 2 tablespoons of oil on each lined pan and spread the oil with your hands.

5 Spoon 1 to 2 tablespoons of the meat mixture directly onto the pan and form it into a circular patty, roughly ¼ inch (6 mm) thick. Continue doing this, leaving 1 inch (2.5 cm) of space between each patty.

6 Place the sheet pans on the bottom rack of the oven and bake for 15 minutes. (If your oven does not fit both pans, bake one pan at a time.) After 15 minutes, check if the bottoms of the patties are cooked; they should look brown and crispy; if not, bake for another 5 minutes. Use a flat spatula to gently flip them over and cook for 10 to 15 minutes longer, until sizzling and golden on both sides. Broil the tops for a few minutes to brown them further if required.

7 Serve as sandwiches in samoon buns or pita bread with sliced tomatoes, green onions, parsley, and mayonnaise, hot sauce, and/or ketchup for topping.

Kofta Bil Tahini

BAKED KOFTA WITH TAHINI

YIELD: 16 kofta; 4 to 6 servings

PREP TIME: 30 minutes

COOK TIME: 30 minutes

◇◇◇◇◇

KOFTA

1 small onion, cut into quarters

1 cup (50 g) packed roughly chopped fresh parsley

4 large cloves garlic, peeled

1½ pounds (680 g) lean ground beef

1½ teaspoons seven spice

1½ teaspoons salt

1 teaspoon paprika

½ teaspoon black pepper

¼ cup (25 g) bread crumbs

2 tablespoons pomegranate molasses

1 tablespoon olive oil

POTATOES

2 small yellow potatoes, peeled

½ teaspoon salt

1 tablespoon olive oil

SAUCE

1 cup (240 ml) tahini

½ cup (120 ml) plain, whole-milk yogurt

¼ cup (60 ml) fresh lemon juice (about 1½ lemons)

1 teaspoon onion powder

½ teaspoon paprika

1 teaspoon salt

2½ cups (600 ml) boiling water

Kofta is a universal food across the Middle Eastern region, not only because it's delicious and easy to make, but also because it's versatile and economical. Transform a pound of ground beef into juicy, well-seasoned kofta and use them in wraps, stews, or sauces with rice. This dish is one variation of the latter application of kofta, and one of my favorite ways to enjoy it. Kofta bil tahini is a traditional Levantine dish that has you pouring a rich tahini sauce all over roasted kofta and potatoes and then digging in with bread, or scooping it on top of rice. In this recipe, the method is streamlined using one large oven-safe skillet to sear the kofta and then roasting the kofta in the oven with the potatoes. The tahini sauce is added and baked for a few minutes just before serving. Tahini is a naturally thick paste, and it will thicken up even more when cooled, so don't worry if it looks thick; that's normal. It's important not to bake the tahini sauce too long to avoid it thickening too much. The crunchy almonds as a garnish are a must!

1 TO MAKE THE KOFTA: Preheat the oven to 450°F (230°C) and position a rack in the middle.

2 Add the onion, parsley, and garlic to a food processor and pulse until chopped very fine. (If you do not have a food processor, you can chop very finely with a knife.) Using your hands, squeeze out as much moisture from the mixture as possible over a bowl.

3 Transfer the mixture to a large bowl, then add the beef, seven spice, 1½ teaspoons salt, 1 teaspoon paprika, black pepper, bread crumbs, pomegranate molasses, and oil. Mix well using your hands, ensuring all the spices are well incorporated. Shape the kofta mixture into 16 equal-sized meatballs; form each meatball into a log shape by elongating it with your fingers.

4 In a 9½-inch (24 cm) round, oven-safe skillet that is 2 inches (5 cm) deep, sear the kofta as you shape them for a few minutes on each side until browned. (Oil is not required for this step.) They do not need to cook all the way through. If you do not have an oven-safe skillet, sear in any skillet then transfer to an oven-safe baking dish.

5 TO MAKE THE POTATOES: Slice the potatoes into ⅛-inch-thick (3 mm) rounds, then cut the rounds in half to form half-moon shapes. Add the potatoes to a small bowl and season with the ½ teaspoon salt and the oil.

CONTINUED ▶

FOR GARNISHING AND SERVING
1 tablespoon olive oil
¼ cup (30 g) slivered almonds
¼ cup (13 g) finely chopped fresh
  parsley
Pita bread or Roz Bi Shaariya
  (page 67)

Note

You can also use only the kofta from this recipe and shape it into logs, patties, or meatballs and then grill them on an outdoor or stovetop grill until cooked through. Use in wraps and bowls with salad and rice. Kofta is freezer-friendly: make a large batch, cook, and then freeze in a freezer bag for a few months.

6 Arrange the kofta all along the outer edge of the skillet, tips facing inward, placing the remaining kofta in the middle. Arrange potato slices, cut sides down, between each kofta, stacking them together as needed to fit them all into the dish.

7 Bake for 25 minutes on the middle rack.

8 MEANWHILE, MAKE THE SAUCE: In a small bowl, whisk together the tahini, yogurt, lemon juice, onion powder, ½ teaspoon paprika, 1 teaspoon salt, and boiling water. The sauce will seize up when the lemon juice is added; keep whisking until it reaches a smooth consistency.

9 After the kofta have baked 25 minutes, remove the skillet from the oven. If baking juices have accumulated, leave them in the skillet. Evenly pour the sauce over the kofta and potatoes and place the skillet back into the oven to bake for 5 to 7 minutes, just until the sauce is heated through and starts to bubble.

10 MEANWHILE, MAKE THE GARNISH: In a small skillet, heat the oil over medium heat, then add the almonds and toast them for a few minutes, or until golden brown, stirring often.

11 Garnish the kofta skillet with the toasted almonds and chopped parsley and serve with pita bread or rice.

Iraqi Mutabbaq Simach
SPICED FISH & RICE

YIELD: 6 servings

PREP TIME: 15 minutes

COOK TIME: 35 minutes

◇◇◇◇◇

SPICE BLEND

1½ tablespoons curry powder

1 tablespoon ground coriander

1 tablespoon paprika

2 teaspoons dried lime powder
  or 2 whole dried limes, crushed

1 teaspoon ground cinnamon

1 teaspoon salt

1 teaspoon ground ginger

FISH

6 skin-on whitefish (such as halibut,
  grouper, catfish, tilapia) fillets
  (2¾ pounds, or 1.25 kg), patted dry

1½ teaspoons salt

2 tablespoons vegetable oil

VERMICELLI NOODLES

1 tablespoon vegetable oil

1 cup (100 g) vermicelli pasta
  noodles, cut into ½-inch (13 mm)
  pieces (if using vermicelli nests,
  break them up by hand)

RICE

1 tablespoon vegetable oil

1 large onion, finely chopped

1½ teaspoons salt

1 cup (145 g) raisins

2 cups (360 g) long-grain white
  basmati rice, rinsed until the water
  runs clear and drained completely

Fish is commonly consumed in Iraq, due to its freshwater rivers, lakes, and marshes being home to a wide variety of fish. Mutabbaq simach is one of the most popular fish dishes, featuring heavily seasoned fish on top of layers of rice and onions, vermicelli noodles, and raisins. The different components are steamed together to infuse the flavors. Typically, bone-in fish pieces are seasoned, fried, and then layered with the rice. In this version, I have adapted the recipe to use boneless fillets, seared and pan-fried separately, and then served on top of the rice. The seasoning mix and the vermicelli topping make this dish truly special.

1 TO MAKE THE SPICE BLEND: In a small bowl, mix together all the spice blend ingredients.

2 TO MAKE THE FISH: In a large bowl or platter, sprinkle both sides of the fillets with the 1½ teaspoons salt, then sprinkle both sides with 2 tablespoons of the spice blend.

3 In a large nonstick pot, heat the 2 tablespoons vegetable oil over medium heat. Add the fish fillets, working in batches to avoid overcrowding, and sear for 1 minute per side, until golden. Continue to cook the fish for 6 to 7 minutes, depending on the thickness, until cooked all the way through; the fish should be opaque and flake easily with a fork. Transfer to a plate.

4 TO MAKE THE VERMICELLI NOODLES: In a small skillet, heat the 1 tablespoon oil over medium heat. Add the noodles and cook, stirring constantly, for 3 to 4 minutes, until the noodles turn a dark golden brown. (Do not stop stirring, as they burn easily.)

5 Add 1 cup (240 ml) of water to the skillet and let the noodles soften for 1 to 2 minutes. The water will make a splashing sound; this is normal. Remove the skillet from the heat, keeping the noodles in it.

6 TO MAKE THE RICE: In the same pot the fish fillets were cooked in, heat the 1 tablespoon vegetable oil over medium heat. Add the onion and cook, stirring often, until softened and lightly golden, 4 to 5 minutes. Add the remaining spice blend and 1½ teaspoons salt to the pot and stir to incorporate. Add the raisins and cook, stirring continuously for 1 minute, then add the vermicelli noodles (and any of their remaining water). Stir to combine everything.

CONTINUED ▶

FOR GARNISHING AND SERVING

½ tablespoon olive oil

½ cup peeled whole (70 g) or slivered (55 g) almonds

Salata (page 44) or Arugula & Pomegranate Salad (page 52)

7 Smooth out the onion-noodle mixture into an even layer in the pot. Add the rice on top, using a wooden spoon to spread it out evenly in the pot. Add 3 cups (720 ml) of water, keeping the heat on medium. The water will come to a low boil within a minute. Let boil for 2 minutes, then immediately cover the pot with a tight-fitting lid and reduce the heat to low. Let the rice cook for 25 minutes, undisturbed.

8 MEANWHILE, MAKE THE GARNISH: In a small skillet, heat the olive oil over low heat, then add the almonds and toast them for 4 to 5 minutes, until golden brown, stirring continuously.

9 After the rice has cooked for 25 minutes, remove the lid and gently fluff it with a fork or wooden spoon and check for doneness. If the rice is soft and fluffy, place the fish pieces over it to heat them, then cover and let stand for 10 minutes; if the rice grains are still firm, splash ¼ cup (60 ml) of water on top, cover, and cook for another 10 minutes over low heat.

10 Once ready to serve, remove the lid and fish pieces and set aside. Place a large tray on top of the pot. (If you do not have a large tray, you can spoon the rice onto a platter.) Using oven mitts, carefully flip the pot upside down while holding the tray firmly in place. When the pot is flipped, gently remove it. If there are some noodles and onions left in the pot, spoon them out and place on top. Place the cooked fish pieces on top and garnish with the toasted almonds. Serve with salad.

Roasted Dukkah-Crusted Trout

YIELD: 4 to 6 servings

PREP TIME: 10 minutes

COOK TIME: 25 minutes

◇◇◇◇◇

1 pound (454 g) red radishes, trimmed and cut in half

1 red onion, cut into ½-inch-thick (13 mm) slices

¾ pound (350 g) asparagus, trimmed

4 tablespoons olive oil, divided

1½ teaspoons kosher salt, divided

1½ pounds (650 g) skin-on rainbow trout fillets (2 large fillets) (or substitute with salmon), rinsed and patted dry

½ recipe Egyptian Dukkah (page 33)

One of the best ways to use Egyptian Dukkah (page 33) is to press it into a large fillet of trout and roast it in the oven. The toasted nuts, seeds, and warm spices elevate an ordinary weeknight fish dinner into a fancy treat. I have also recently been quite taken with roasted radish. Radishes are commonly consumed in the Middle East, but only when fresh, for their crunch and peppery flavor. Roasting them is a technique I picked up here in the West that completely transforms them, mellowing their sharpness and enhancing their natural sweetness.

1 Preheat the oven to 400°F (205°C). Line a large, rimmed sheet pan with parchment paper.

2 Place the radishes, onion, and asparagus on the prepared sheet pan and toss with 2 tablespoons of the oil and 1 teaspoon of the salt. Bake for 10 minutes.

3 Meanwhile, place the trout fillets on a flat surface and drizzle each one with 1 tablespoon of oil, then sprinkle each one with ½ teaspoon of salt. Sprinkle each fillet with 4 or 5 teaspoons of the Egyptian dukkah, covering the whole surface and rubbing the seasoning into the fish.

4 After the vegetables have baked for 10 minutes, remove the sheet pan from the oven and add the trout fillets. Place back into the oven and bake for 15 minutes longer, or until the fish is flaky and cooked through.

5 Serve the fish with the asparagus, radishes, and onion.

Loubia Bil Zeit

OLIVE OIL–BRAISED GREEN BEANS

YIELD: 4 servings
PREP TIME: 10 minutes
COOK TIME: 30 minutes

◇◇◇◇◇

¼ cup (60 ml) olive oil

1 large onion, finely chopped

12 large cloves garlic, roughly
   chopped

1½ teaspoons kosher salt, divided

1 pound (454 g) green beans
   (see Note), trimmed and cut
   in half crosswise

¼ teaspoon black pepper

2 small vine tomatoes, diced

1 tablespoon tomato paste

FOR GARNISHING AND SERVING

Olive oil

Kosher salt (optional)

Pita bread or Roz Bi Shaariya
   (page 67)

This vegetarian main dish is made with green beans, long beans, or flat Romano beans and is common across Levantine countries. It can also be served as a cold appetizer. The beans are braised with lots of olive oil, garlic, and tomatoes and enjoyed scooped up with bread. The simplicity of this dish is what makes it special, and the simple ingredients make the green beans shine. This is a great light weeknight dinner, and I also love serving it cold the next day.

1 In a large nonstick skillet, heat the oil over medium heat. Add the onion and cook, stirring often, until softened, 6 to 7 minutes.

2 Add the garlic and 1 teaspoon of the salt and continue to cook and stir for 1 to 2 minutes, until the garlic is fragrant.

3 Add the green beans, remaining ½ teaspoon salt, and pepper. Cook and stir for 2 to 3 minutes, then cover with a tight-fitting lid, reduce the heat to medium-low, and let cook for 6 to 7 minutes, stirring occasionally.

4 Remove the lid and add the tomatoes, tomato paste, and 3 or 4 tablespoons of water. Stir to combine, then cover again and cook for 10 minutes longer, stirring occasionally, until they reach a crisp, tender texture. Remove from the heat.

5 Transfer the beans to a flat plate, pouring all the pan juices as well. Drizzle with olive oil and an extra sprinkling of salt, if desired. Serve with a side of pita bread or rice.

Note

This dish is typically cooked using long green beans as well as Romano beans. It works with most green bean varieties, provided you adjust the cooking time of the beans and use more liquid if necessary.

Main Dishes Worth the Effort

Mom's Stuffed Chicken

YIELD: 6 servings

PREP TIME: 25 minutes

COOK TIME: 1 hour and 30 minutes

◇◇◇◇◇

CHICKEN

1 whole chicken (4 to 4½ pounds
or 2 kg), patted dry

4 teaspoons kosher salt

2 tablespoons onion powder

2 tablespoons garlic powder

1 tablespoon curry powder

1 tablespoon dried lime powder
(or substitute 1 tablespoon
fresh lemon juice)

1 teaspoon ground allspice

½ teaspoon ground cinnamon

1½ teaspoons black pepper

¾ cup (180 ml) barbecue sauce

VEGETABLES

4 small yellow potatoes, peeled

2 large onions, peeled

1 teaspoon kosher salt

RICE STUFFING

⅔ pound (300 g) regular ground
beef

1 teaspoon ground allspice

½ teaspoon ground cinnamon

4 teaspoons kosher salt, divided

½ teaspoon black pepper

1 cup (135 g) frozen peas

1 cup (145 g) raisins

2 cups (410 g) long-grain white
basmati rice, rinsed until the water
runs clear and drained completely

Along with Maqluba (page 181), Biryani (page 122), and Dolma (page 169), this is another one of my mom's irresistible dishes. Stuffing chicken with a mixture of rice and ground beef and roasting it to perfection is a common way of presenting whole chicken across Middle Eastern countries. But this recipe is extra special because it has my mom's specific blend of sauce and spices, and it really can't be topped. My mom is a creative cook; she tends to stray every once in a while and do her own thing. Case in point: The addition of barbecue sauce to the marinade in this recipe. There's no such thing as barbecue sauce in Middle Eastern cuisine! But it works so well here, along with an array of spices, including dried lime powder. While it may seem complex, this is a recipe I'd recommend for beginner cooks who want to make something impressive. It's hard to mess up. The rice ends up absorbing all the chicken juices—I like it even more than the chicken. My mom would make this whenever we all gathered together, and we would be fighting over who gets more of the juicy rice from inside the chicken.

1 Preheat the oven to 400°F (205°C); place a rack in the middle and remove any racks above it.

2 TO MAKE THE CHICKEN: Place the chicken on a large tray or platter and season it with the 4 teaspoons salt, covering the entire surface, inside and out.

3 In a small bowl, mix together the onion powder, garlic powder, curry powder, lime powder, allspice, cinnamon, 1½ teaspoons pepper, and barbecue sauce. Set aside 2 tablespoons of the marinade for the vegetables, then slather the rest all over the chicken, including inside and under the skin that covers the breast by gently placing your fingers under the skin, slowly pushing to slightly separate it, and adding the marinade in between.

4 TO MAKE THE VEGETABLES: Cut the potatoes into quarters to form 4 large wedges, then rotate the wedges 90 degrees and cut once across to create 8 large chunks. Repeat with the onion. Place the potatoes and onions in a large bowl and season with the 1 teaspoon salt and reserved marinade.

CONTINUED ▶

5 TO MAKE THE RICE STUFFING: Heat a medium nonstick pot or large skillet over medium heat. Add the ground beef and cook, breaking it up into small pieces with a wooden spoon, for 5 to 7 minutes, until browned. Add the allspice, cinnamon, 1 teaspoon of the salt, and the ½ teaspoon pepper and mix well. Continue to cook for 3 to 5 minutes, until all the meat juices dry up. Mix in the peas and raisins, then add the rice, the remaining 3 teaspoons salt, and 4 cups (960 ml) of water. Gently mix the rice into the meat mixture and bring to a boil over medium heat. Let cook, uncovered, at a gentle boil for about 7 minutes, or until all the water is absorbed but the rice looks moist. Remove from the heat. (The rice is only half-cooked at this point.) Let cool for a few minutes.

6 In a chicken roaster with a lid, place the potatoes and onions on the bottom in a single layer. (If you do not have a roaster with a lid, use a large enough baking dish and aluminum foil to cover it tightly.)

7 To stuff the chicken, spoon some of the rice-beef mixture into the cavity of the chicken until it is full. Use a few toothpicks to close the cavity by folding the skin flaps over each other and threading the toothpick through both layers of skin, then threading it back out to hold in place. Leave the remaining stuffing in the pot.

8 Place the stuffed chicken in the roaster on top of the vegetables. Cover with the lid, place on the middle rack in the oven, and bake for 1 hour. Remove the pan from the oven and open the lid. Spoon the rest of the rice stuffing inside the pan, trying your best to place it on the bottom with the vegetables on top. Close the pan, place it back into the oven, and bake for another 30 to 40 minutes, until the chicken is fully cooked (white on the inside or has an internal temperature of 165°F, or 74°C).

9 Let the stuffed chicken sit for 10 to 15 minutes before serving. You can serve it right from the roaster or transfer to a platter.

Yemeni Chicken Mandi

YIELD: 4 to 6 servings

PREP TIME: 15 minutes

COOK TIME: 1 hour and 15 minutes

◇◇◇◇◇

CHICKEN

1 teaspoon ground coriander

1 teaspoon ground cumin

½ teaspoon ground cloves

½ teaspoon ground cardamom

½ teaspoon ground cinnamon

½ teaspoon black pepper

1 teaspoon turmeric, divided

2½ teaspoons kosher salt, divided

1 whole chicken (about 4 pounds, or 1.8 kg), cut into quarters

4 tablespoons olive oil, divided

1 medium yellow onion, finely chopped

2½ cups (500 g) long-grain white basmati rice, rinsed until the water runs clear and drained completely

CRISPY ONIONS

Vegetable oil

4 small yellow onions, cut in half and thinly sliced into half-moons (use a sharp knife, mandoline, or a food processor with a slicer attachment)

½ teaspoon kosher salt

Yemeni chicken mandi is a rice dish that has gained popularity not only in Yemen, but across all the Arab world. It can be made with lamb or chicken, and it is heavily spiced with Yemeni hawaij spices—a classic blend of aromatic spices used across Yemeni cuisine. Traditionally, mandi is cooked in an underground oven called a *taboon*, using hot coals. This recipe is an easier adaptation of the dish, suitable for a modern kitchen. The seasoned chicken sits on top of glistening yellow rice, garnished with fried onions, almonds, and raisins. It is commonly served with a spicy green or red *bisbas* sauce, which resembles a spicy chutney.

1 TO MAKE THE CHICKEN: Preheat the oven to 450°F (230°C). Line a large, rimmed sheet pan with parchment paper.

2 In a small bowl, mix the coriander, cumin, cloves, cardamom, cinnamon, black pepper, ½ teaspoon of the turmeric, and 1 teaspoon of the salt until well combined. Reserve 1½ tablespoons of the spice mixture for the rice later.

3 Pat the chicken pieces dry with a paper towel and place them on the prepared sheet pan. Drizzle 1 tablespoon of olive oil all over the chicken pieces, then sprinkle with the spice mixture, rubbing the spices into the chicken and ensuring all sides are covered.

4 In a large, deep skillet, heat 1 tablespoon of the olive oil over medium heat for 1 minute. Add the chicken and sear for 2 minutes per side on all sides, or until lightly golden. Transfer the chicken to the sheet pan, then bake in the oven for 45 minutes, or until cooked (white on the inside or has an internal temperature of 165°F, or 74°C). Broil the chicken for 4 to 5 minutes, until deeply golden.

5 In the same skillet that the chicken was seared in, add the remaining 2 tablespoons olive oil and heat for 1 minute over medium heat. Add the chopped onion and cook, stirring often, for 4 to 5 minutes, until softened. Add the reserved spice mixture and the remaining ½ teaspoon turmeric and 1½ teaspoons salt. Stir into the onion and cook for 1 to 2 minutes. Add the rice and stir to combine. Add 3½ cups (840 ml) of water and bring to a boil over medium-high heat. Once boiling, reduce the heat to low and cover with the lid. Let cook for 20 minutes, undisturbed.

CONTINUED ▶

FOR GARNISHING

¼ cup (30 g) slivered almonds

¼ cup (35 g) raisins

BISBAS SAUCE

1 large jalapeño, or more to taste

2 cloves garlic, peeled

½ cup (20 g) packed roughly
  chopped fresh cilantro

½ cup (25 g) packed roughly chopped
  fresh parsley

2 tablespoons olive oil

½ teaspoon kosher salt, plus more
  if needed

¼ teaspoon ground cumin

Juice of ½ lemon

6 MEANWHILE, MAKE THE CRISPY ONIONS: In a large skillet, heat enough vegetable oil (at least ½ cup, or 120 ml) over medium-high heat to cover the sliced onions. Add the onions so that they are immersed in the oil and not overcrowded, working in two batches, and cook until the edges start to turn golden. Gently bring the outer ones to the center and continue frying until they all turn golden brown; be careful not to burn them. With a slotted spoon, remove the onions to a paper towel–lined tray to absorb the excess oil. Sprinkle with the ½ teaspoon salt.

7 TO MAKE THE GARNISH: Using the onion oil left over in the skillet, toast the almonds over medium heat for 4 to 5 minutes, until golden, stirring continuously. Transfer to a small bowl. Add the raisins to the same skillet and stir for 30 seconds until they are warm and glossy. Transfer them to the bowl with the almonds.

8 TO MAKE THE BISBAS SAUCE: Add all the sauce ingredients to a small food processor and pulse for a few minutes until a thick paste. Taste and adjust for salt if needed.

9 After the rice has cooked for 20 minutes, fluff with a fork or wooden spoon. Spoon onto a large platter and top with a layer of crispy onions. Add the chicken pieces, then garnish with the toasted almonds and raisins. Serve with the bisbas sauce and more crispy onions on the side.

Chicken & Freekeh Casserole

YIELD: 4 to 6 servings

PREP TIME: 10 minutes

COOK TIME: 1 hour and 30 minutes

◇◇◇◇◇

CHICKEN

¼ cup (60 ml) fresh lemon juice

5 large cloves garlic, crushed

4 teaspoons seven spice

2½ teaspoons salt

½ teaspoon black pepper

4½ pounds (2 kg) bone-in, skin-on
   chicken leg quarters (5 leg quarters)

CARROTS

⅔ pound (300 g) small or medium
   carrots, peeled and kept whole if
   small or cut in half lengthwise
   if large

½ teaspoon salt

¼ teaspoon black pepper

1 tablespoon olive oil

FREEKEH

2 tablespoons olive oil

1 large onion, finely chopped

2½ cups (350 g) whole or cracked
   freekeh, rinsed and drained
   (see Note)

1 teaspoon seven spice

1½ teaspoons kosher salt

4 cups (960 ml) chicken broth or
   water

FOR SERVING

Salata (page 44) or Arugula &
   Pomegranate Salad (page 52)

Note

Some freekeh varieties contain
debris and small rocks, so as
you rinse it, pick them out.

Freekeh (also referred to as "freek") is a common grain used in Levantine and Egyptian cuisine. Known for its nutty and smoky flavor and chewy texture, it is a young green wheat that is roasted and cracked. It is often cooked as a pilaf, mixed into salads, or used to stuff seasoned and roasted chicken. This recipe is a nod to the traditional stuffed chicken dish but uses chicken leg quarters for quicker cooking. I can't rave enough about how flavorful the freekeh ends up tasting.

1 TO MAKE THE CHICKEN: Preheat the oven to 400°F (205°C).

2 In a large bowl, mix together the lemon juice, garlic, seven spice, 2½ teaspoons salt, and ½ teaspoon pepper.

3 Make three or four ½-inch (13 mm) slits on the bottom side of each chicken quarter. Add the chicken quarters to the bowl with the marinade and slather the chicken with the marinade, making sure to cover all sides and working it under the skin. Let sit for 10 to 15 minutes, or marinate, covered, in the refrigerator overnight.

4 MEANWHILE, PREP THE CARROTS: In a medium bowl, mix the carrots with the ½ teaspoon salt, ¼ teaspoon pepper, and 1 tablespoon oil.

5 TO MAKE THE FREEKEH: In a large roasting pan that is also stovetop safe, heat the 2 tablespoons oil over medium heat. (If you don't have a stovetop-safe roaster, you can use a large skillet then transfer everything to a baking dish.) Sear the chicken leg quarters skin side down for 2 to 3 minutes until golden. Flip and sear the other side for a few minutes. Transfer to a plate.

6 Add the onion to the roasting pan and cook, stirring often, until softened, 2 to 3 minutes. Add the freekeh and toast while stirring for 2 to 3 minutes. Add the seven spice and 1½ teaspoons salt and cook, stirring often, for a few minutes. Add the broth and bring to a boil. Once the water is boiling, nestle the chicken quarters on top of the freekeh and scatter the carrots throughout.

7 Tightly cover the roasting pan with aluminum foil and bake for 1 hour. After 1 hour, uncover the pan and bake for another 30 minutes, or until the chicken is fully cooked (white on the inside or has an internal temperature of 165°F, or 74°C) and the freekeh is tender. Broil for 3 to 5 minutes, until the chicken skin is golden brown.

8 Serve with salad.

Lebanese Lemon-Garlic Spatchcock Chicken

YIELD: 6 servings

PREP TIME: 10 minutes

COOK TIME: 45 minutes

◇◇◇◇◇

GARLIC-BUTTER OIL

¼ cup (60 g) unsalted butter

¼ cup (60 ml) olive oil

12 large garlic cloves, crushed

CHICKEN

3½ teaspoons kosher salt

1 teaspoon black pepper

1 teaspoon onion powder

1 teaspoon garlic powder

1 teaspoon dried basil

1 whole chicken (3⅓ to 4½ pounds, or 1.5 to 2 kg), spatchcocked (see Note on page 168)

POTATOES

4 large yellow potatoes, cut into eighths

1 teaspoon kosher salt

½ teaspoon black pepper

¼ cup (60 ml) chicken broth

BAKING LIQUID

¾ cup (180 ml) chicken broth

⅔ cup (160 ml) fresh lemon juice

Once you learn how to spatchcock a chicken, it may be the only way you cook it going forward. Spatchcocking a chicken has so many benefits, including a much faster cooking time than a whole chicken, more even cooking (because the chicken lies flat), and crispier skin (because all the skin is exposed to the heat in a flat layer). This recipe uses a classic lemon-garlic flavor combination. And I really mean business when I say "lemon-garlic," because this chicken will be extra lemony and extra garlicky. The technique used to roast the chicken yields extra juices on the bottom of the pan, perfect for scooping over the chicken and potatoes and mopping up with bread.

1 Preheat the oven to 450°F (230°C) and position a rack on the bottom.

2 TO MAKE THE GARLIC-BUTTER OIL: In a medium microwave-safe glass bowl, melt the butter in a microwave. Add the olive oil and crushed garlic and mix well to combine.

3 TO MAKE THE CHICKEN: In a medium bowl, combine the 3½ teaspoons salt, 1 teaspoon pepper, onion powder, garlic powder, basil, and 5 tablespoons of the garlic-butter oil and mix to form a thick paste.

4 Place the chicken on a cutting board and pat it dry. Slather the seasoning paste all over the chicken, covering the whole surface and working it under the skin. If you have the time, place the chicken in a bowl, cover, and let marinate for a few hours in the refrigerator, then bring it to room temperature for 30 minutes before cooking; otherwise, you can continue with the recipe without letting the chicken marinate.

5 TO MAKE THE POTATOES: Place the potatoes in a large roasting tray (at least 9 x 13 inches, or 22 x 33 cm, and 2 inches, or 5 cm, deep) and sprinkle them with the 1 teaspoon salt and ½ teaspoon pepper. Add 2 tablespoons of the garlic-butter oil and toss to combine.

6 If you have a rack that fits over the roasting tray, place it on top of the potatoes, then place the chicken, skin side up, on the rack; if you don't have a rack, place the chicken directly on the potatoes, skin side up. (The rack helps achieve a crispier chicken.)

7 Pour ¼ cup (60 ml) broth in the bottom of the pan, then place the pan in the oven on the bottom rack. Bake for 30 minutes.

CONTINUED ▶

8 MEANWHILE, MAKE THE BAKING LIQUID: In a medium bowl, combine the remaining garlic-butter oil, the lemon juice, and ¾ cup (180 ml) broth and mix well.

9 After the chicken has baked for 30 minutes, pour the baking liquid all over the chicken and potatoes. Continue to bake for another 15 to 20 minutes, until the chicken is fully cooked and golden brown (white on the inside or has an internal temperature of 165°F, or 74°C). If required, broil the chicken for 4 to 5 minutes to get more color. Let rest for 10 minutes before serving.

Note

To spatchcock a chicken, place it on a large cutting board, breast side down, with the neck facing toward you. Using kitchen shears and holding the neck in one hand, cut along one side of the spine, separating it from the ribs. Cut close to the spine so that you do not remove any excess meat. Continue to cut about three-quarters along the spine on one side, then repeat on the other side of the spine. Hold the spine for leverage and continue cutting on both sides to remove it completely. Flip the chicken over and use the palm of your hand to press down gently and firmly over the breast, flattening the chicken. You can save the spine to make chicken stock. You can also ask your butcher to spatchcock the chicken for you.

Onion Dolma
STUFFED ONIONS

YIELD: 6 servings
PREP TIME: 30 minutes
COOK TIME: 1 hour and 30 minutes

◇◇◇◇◇

DOLMA
8 small, oval-shaped yellow onions (see Notes on page 171)

⅔ pound (300 g) lean ground beef

4 large cloves garlic, minced

½ yellow onion, small diced

½ large red bell pepper, small diced

1½ cups (300 g) short-grain white rice, rinsed until the water runs clear and drained completely

½ cup (25 g) finely chopped fresh parsley

2 teaspoons kosher salt

½ teaspoon black pepper

½ teaspoon ground cumin

1 teaspoon ground allspice

1 teaspoon dried dill

1 teaspoon dried mint

3 tablespoons pomegranate molasses

3 tablespoons tomato paste

2 tablespoons fresh lemon juice

BAKING LIQUID
½ cup (120 g) tomato paste

3 tablespoons pomegranate molasses

¼ cup (60 ml) fresh lemon juice

1½ teaspoons kosher salt

½ teaspoon black pepper

4 cups (960 ml) hot water

FOR SERVING
Salata (page 44)

Plain, whole-milk yogurt

This dish is one I came up with as my "cheat dolma." Authentic Iraqi dolma, the way my mom makes it, uses an array of vegetables, such as grape leaves, Swiss chard, eggplant, zucchini, tomatoes, and peppers. All these vegetables are cored and stuffed, which takes hours. As a way of enjoying dolma more often, I decided to start making it using only onions, because they are the easiest to stuff by far! The results are nothing short of amazing, with the onions turning sweet and melting in your mouth, the tangy filling creating a perfect contrast to the sweetness. You won't find me making authentic dolma more than maybe twice a year, but this dish—this I make monthly, at least!

1 Preheat the oven to 450°F (230°C) and position a rack on the bottom level.

2 TO MAKE THE DOLMA: Peel an onion without slicing off the ends, then, using a paring knife, dig around the end where the root is and carve it out slightly, about ¼ inch (6 mm) deep (this helps separate the layers). After doing this, discard the root and separate all the layers slightly at the end to expose them. Make a long cut along the length of the onion through all the layers to the center; do not cut past the center. Repeat with the remaining onions. Place the onions in a medium microwave-safe glass bowl and microwave for 1 minute to soften the layers slightly (you can also boil them on the stovetop for 1 minute). Let cool while you prepare the rest of the ingredients.

3 In a large bowl, combine the ground beef, garlic, chopped onion, red pepper, rice, parsley, 2 teaspoons salt, black pepper, cumin, allspice, dried dill, dried mint, pomegranate molasses, 3 tablespoons tomato paste, and 2 tablespoons lemon juice and mix well.

4 To stuff the onions, use your fingers to carefully dislodge every layer of each onion and pop them out, one by one. Gently pry the layers apart from both sides until you reach the center. Repeat with the remaining onions until you have them all in single layers. Place roughly 2 tablespoons of the stuffing inside each onion layer, then roll it closed. The ends of the onion should fold over one another by at least ½ inch (13 mm); if you cannot do this, it means you have stuffed it too much. Place the stuffed onions in a 9 x 13-inch (23 x 33 cm) baking dish, packed tightly side by side with the seam sides down, to help them stay closed; they should be snuggly packed in.

CONTINUED ▶

5 TO MAKE THE BAKING LIQUID: In a medium, heatproof glass bowl or measuring cup, combine the ½ cup (120 g) tomato paste, pomegranate molasses, ¼ cup (60 ml) lemon juice, 1½ teaspoons salt, and black pepper. Add the hot water and mix everything together.

6 Pour the sauce all over the onions. Tightly cover the dish with aluminum foil and bake for 1½ hours. After 1 hour, check the onions to ensure there is enough liquid for them to continue cooking. There should be at least 1 inch (2.5 cm) of liquid in the dish; if needed, add another ½ cup (120 ml) of water. Remove the stuffed onions when both the rice and onions are very soft. Let cool for 10 minutes before serving.

7 Serve with salad and yogurt.

Notes

+ Using oval-shaped yellow onions makes it easier to pry apart the layers. If you can't find oval ones, round ones will work too.

+ If you have leftover filling, you may also stuff mini sweet peppers. Slice the tops off the peppers, then use your fingers to remove any seeds. Stuff them and then add them to the baking dish with the onions.

+ To make this dish vegetarian, skip the ground beef in the filling and follow the recipe as directed.

Sticky Pomegranate Short Ribs

YIELD: 4 to 6 servings
PREP TIME: 10 minutes
COOK TIME: 3 hours and 30 minutes

◇◇◇◇◇

4½ pounds (2 kg) bone-in short ribs
1½ teaspoons kosher salt
½ teaspoon black pepper
2 tablespoons vegetable oil
1 large onion, finely chopped
¼ cup (60 ml) ketchup
½ cup (120 ml) pomegranate molasses
2 tablespoons soy sauce
6 large cloves garlic, minced
Juice of 1 lemon
1 teaspoon ground cumin
1 teaspoon paprika

FOR GARNISHING AND SERVING
Microgreens or fresh parsley and mint leaves
Pomegranate arils
Tahini Cabbage Slaw (page 48) (optional)
Roz Asfar (page 71) (optional)

Beef short ribs are not commonly used in Middle Eastern cuisine. I wasn't introduced to them until after I moved to Canada. When I first tried them, I was quite surprised that beef could yield such a meltingly delicious result resembling that of lamb. So naturally I loved experimenting with them. The key thing about great short ribs is to braise them at a low temperature for an extended period of time to allow the collagen to break down into gelatin, resulting in fall-off-the-bone texture. The marinade I use in this recipe is a mixture of ketchup and pomegranate molasses, a combination often used in Iraqi-style marinades, with a touch of soy sauce to balance the flavors. The result is sticky, sweet-and-sour short ribs that will please any crowd.

1 To make the short ribs: Preheat the oven to 300°F (150°C). Season each short rib with salt and black pepper.

2 In a large Dutch oven or oven-safe pot, heat the oil over medium-high heat. Add the short ribs, working in batches to avoid overcrowding, and sear on all sides until browned. Transfer to a plate. Remove any excess fat from the pot and discard it.

3 Add the onion to the same pot and cook, stirring often, until softened and translucent, 5 to 7 minutes.

4 While the onion cooks, combine the ketchup, pomegranate molasses, soy sauce, garlic, lemon juice, cumin, and paprika with 1 cup (240 ml) of water in a medium bowl and mix well. Pour this mixture into the pot with the onion and bring to a simmer. Taste and adjust for salt if necessary.

5 Place the short ribs back into the pot and stir to coat the ribs in the onions and sauce. Cover with the lid or aluminum foil, and bake for 3 hours, or until fork-tender, then uncover and return to the oven for another 10 to 15 minutes to brown the tops.

6 Transfer the short ribs to a serving dish. Remove excess fat from the pot by scooping it out or layering a paper towel on top to absorb it, then discard.

7 Let the sauce in the pot simmer for 10 to 15 minutes, until thickened, then brush it on top of the short ribs and serve the rest on the side.

8 Garnish with microgreens or fresh parsley and mint and pomegranate arils and serve with slaw (if using) and rice (if using).

Sheikh El Mahshi
STUFFED EGGPLANT BOATS

YIELD: 6 servings

PREP TIME: 15 minutes

COOK TIME: 1 hour and 30 minutes

◇◇◇◇◇

EGGPLANT

¼ cup (60 ml) olive oil

9 Indian eggplants (or substitute 6 Italian eggplants or 3 American eggplants) (about 2¼ pounds, or 1 kg total), with the ends intact and peeled lengthwise every other stripe in a zebra pattern

1 teaspoon kosher salt

BEEF FILLING

2 tablespoons olive oil

½ large onion, finely chopped

1½ pounds (700 g) lean ground beef

1½ teaspoons ground allspice

1 teaspoon ground cinnamon

½ teaspoon black pepper

1½ teaspoons kosher salt

SAUCE

2 cups (480 ml) tomato passata (puree)

½ teaspoon kosher salt

¼ teaspoon black pepper

2 tablespoons pomegranate molasses

FOR GARNISHING AND SERVING

¼ cup (13 g) finely chopped fresh parsley

Roz Bi Shaariya (page 67)

Salata (page 44)

The term *sheikh* is a title used to refer to a respected elder, and *mahshi* means "stuffed." This dish translates to "the leader of all stuffed dishes," and I am in full agreement, because this dish is absolutely superior! My mom also stuffs onions and zucchini. To cut time, I use only eggplant, but I do sometimes throw in a few stuffed onions (learn how to core and stuff an onion in the Onion Dolma recipe on page 169). The not-so-secret ingredient in the sauce is the pomegranate molasses.

1 TO MAKE THE EGGPLANT: Preheat the oven to 450°F (230°C). In a large, oven-safe skillet, heat the ¼ cup (60 ml) oil for a few minutes over medium-high heat. Add the eggplants, working in batches to avoid overcrowding, and sear on all sides for 3 to 4 minutes, until lightly golden. Arrange all the seared eggplants in the skillet, add 1 cup (240 ml) of water, and cover. Bake for 40 to 45 minutes, until fork-tender.

2 MEANWHILE, MAKE THE BEEF FILLING: In a large skillet, heat the 2 tablespoons oil over medium heat. Add the onion and cook, stirring often, until softened and translucent, 5 to 6 minutes. Add the ground beef and cook, breaking it up into small pieces with a wooden spoon, for 6 to 7 minutes, until browned. Add the allspice, cinnamon, ½ teaspoon pepper, and 1½ teaspoons salt and mix to combine. Cook for 5 to 8 minutes longer, until the meat juices dry up. Remove from the heat.

3 TO MAKE THE SAUCE: In a large bowl, mix the passata, ½ teaspoon salt, ¼ teaspoon pepper, and pomegranate molasses with 1 cup (240 ml) of water until combined.

4 Remove the fork-tender eggplants from the oven, leaving the oven on. Make a cut halfway deep along the length of each eggplant, stopping just before the bottom and leaving the ends intact, to create a boat shape. Using a fork, pry the eggplants open and gently mash up and push down the insides to make space for the filling. Sprinkle the 1 teaspoon salt among the eggplants to season the insides. Scoop a few tablespoons of the filling into each eggplant boat, filling it as much as possible. You can also spoon leftover filling into the skillet around the eggplants. Pour the sauce over the eggplants, ensuring that some of the sauce is on top.

5 Bake, uncovered, for 15 to 20 minutes, until the liquid is bubbling. If required, add ½ cup (120 ml) of water to the pan to create enough of a thick sauce to spoon over rice. Garnish with the chopped parsley and serve with rice and salad.

Eggplant & Potato Moussaka

YIELD: 6 servings

PREP TIME: 20 minutes

COOK TIME: 1 hour and 10 minutes

◇◇◇◇◇

EGGPLANT

2 large American (globe) eggplants (2½ pounds, or 1.2 kg), ends trimmed, peeled lengthwise every other stripe in a zebra pattern, and cut into ¼-inch-thick (6 mm) rounds

½ teaspoon kosher salt

¼ cup (60 ml) olive oil

POTATOES

3⅓ pounds (1.5 kg) russet or Yukon gold potatoes, peeled and cut into large pieces (roughly into eighths)

¼ cup (55 g) salted butter

1 teaspoon kosher salt, plus more if needed

¼ teaspoon black pepper, plus more if needed

1 cup (240 ml) whole milk, divided

FILLING

2 tablespoons vegetable oil

1 large onion, finely diced

4 cloves garlic, minced

1½ pounds (680 g) lean ground beef

1 teaspoon kosher salt

½ teaspoon black pepper

3 tablespoons finely chopped fresh thyme (or substitute with 2 tablespoons dried oregano or basil)

1 teaspoon onion powder

1 teaspoon garlic powder

1½ cups (375 g) tomato passata (puree)

This is not your typical Greek-style moussaka made with bechamel sauce. This moussaka has somehow evolved over time in my husband's family and become a staple for us. It is a cross between moussaka and shepherd's pie, bringing together the best of both dishes. It was one of the first recipes I shared on the blog that went viral.

1 Preheat the oven to 450°F (230°C) and place a rack in the middle.

2 TO MAKE THE EGGPLANT: Place the eggplant in a single layer on a large, rimmed sheet pan lined with parchment paper and sprinkle with ½ teaspoon salt and drizzle with the olive oil. (Use two sheet pans if necessary.) Bake for 40 minutes, or until golden and softened.

3 TO MAKE THE POTATOES: Place the potatoes in a large pot over high heat and cover with cold water. Bring to a boil and cook until very soft, 20 to 25 minutes. Drain and leave the potatoes in the pot. Add the butter, 1 teaspoon salt, ¼ teaspoon pepper, and 1 cup (240 ml) milk. Mash the potatoes using a potato masher or ricer until creamy and fluffy.

4 WHILE THE EGGPLANT AND POTATOES COOK, MAKE THE FILLING: In a large skillet, heat the vegetable oil over medium heat. Add the onion and cook, stirring often, until softened and translucent, 5 to 7 minutes. Add the garlic and cook for another minute, stirring often. Add the ground beef and cook, breaking it up into small pieces with a wooden spoon, for 5 to 7 minutes, until browned. Add the salt, pepper, thyme, and onion and garlic powders and oregano and stir. Cook for 2 to 3 minutes until the meat juices dry up. Add the passata and stir to combine. Remove from the heat.

5 In a 9 x 13-inch (23 x 33 cm) baking dish, layer all the baked eggplant to cover the base of the dish, overlapping the pieces as necessary. Spread all the beef mixture evenly on top. Spoon the mashed potatoes on top, adding large spoonfuls to cover the surface, then use a flat or offset spatula to smooth the potatoes into an even layer. Ensure all the edges are sealed with the potato.

6 Use a fork and run it all along the surface of the potatoes in rows, pressing down gently to make grooves. Bake for 30 minutes. Spray the surface of the baking dish with oil, then broil for 2 minutes to brown the top slightly. Let cool for 10 minutes before slicing and serving.

Iraqi Tapsi Betenjan
EGGPLANT CASSEROLE

YIELD: 6 servings
PREP TIME: 20 minutes
COOK TIME: 1 hour and 45 minutes

◇◇◇◇◇

EGGPLANT AND POTATOES

3 large yellow potatoes, peeled and sliced into ¼-inch-thick (6 mm) rounds

1 teaspoon kosher salt, divided

3 tablespoons olive oil, divided

2 large eggplants, ends trimmed, peeled lengthwise every other stripe in a zebra pattern, and sliced into ¼-inch-thick (6 mm) rounds

BEEF AND OTHER VEGETABLES

2 tablespoons olive oil, divided

1½ pounds (700 g) lean ground beef

1½ teaspoons kosher salt, divided

1½ teaspoons ground allspice

½ teaspoon black pepper

1 tablespoon tomato paste

1 tablespoon pomegranate molasses

1 large yellow onion, cut in half and thinly sliced into half-moons

1 large red bell pepper, cut in half, seeds and stems removed, and cut into half-circles

1 large tomato, sliced ¼ inch (6 mm) thick

If you were to ask my husband and me what our last meal on Earth would be, you may get tapsi betenjan as the answer. This dish is quintessential Iraqi comfort food. Fans of eggplant will rejoice at its eggplant-centric flavor; it really would not be the same without it. This casserole is made by layering beef kofta, fried eggplant, and often fried potatoes, onions, and peppers and baking them in a rich tomato sauce laden with pomegranate molasses. The pomegranate molasses gives this dish the classic sweet-and-sour flavor that Iraqi dishes are known for. The result is a tangy and saucy casserole that is scooped over a plate of white rice or enjoyed with Iraqi bread. Traditionally, the beef is shaped into patties, but I usually just layer ground beef to save time. Also, instead of frying the eggplant and potatoes, I find roasting them until golden to be a lighter and quicker alternative without sacrificing flavor.

1 Preheat the oven to 450°F (230°C) using the convection setting and place a rack in the middle. (If you don't have a convection setting, use the bake setting.) Line two large, rimmed sheet pans with parchment paper.

2 TO MAKE THE EGGPLANT AND POTATOES: Place the potatoes in one of the prepared sheet pans and sprinkle with ½ teaspoon of the salt and drizzle with 1 tablespoon of the oil. Spread the potatoes into a single layer (some overlap is fine). In the second prepared sheet pan, place the eggplant and sprinkle with the remaining ½ teaspoon salt and drizzle with the remaining 2 tablespoons oil. Spread the eggplant into a single layer (some overlap is fine). Bake both pans for 40 minutes, or until the eggplant is golden and the potatoes start to soften.

3 MEANWHILE, MAKE THE BEEF AND OTHER VEGETABLES: In a large skillet, heat 1 tablespoon of the oil over medium heat for 1 minute. Add the ground beef and cook, breaking it up into small pieces with a wooden spoon, for 5 to 7 minutes, until browned. Add 1 teaspoon of the salt, the allspice, ¼ teaspoon black pepper, 1 tablespoon tomato paste, and 1 tablespoon pomegranate molasses and mix well. Transfer to a plate.

4 To the same skillet, add the remaining 1 tablespoon oil, onion, and red pepper. Season with the remaining ½ teaspoon salt, and cook, stirring often, over medium heat for 5 to 7 minutes, until softened.

CONTINUED ▶

COOKING LIQUID

2½ cups (600 ml) boiling water

1 teaspoon salt

½ teaspoon black pepper

2 tablespoons pomegranate
  molasses

5 tablespoons tomato paste

FOR GARNISHING AND SERVING

Finely chopped fresh parsley
  (optional)

Roz Bi Shaariya (page 67)

Salata (page 44)

5 TO MAKE THE COOKING LIQUID: In a medium bowl, mix all the cooking liquid ingredients until combined well.

6 When the eggplant and potatoes are done, remove them from the oven, keeping the oven on. Spoon the ground beef into a 9 x 13-inch (23 x 33 cm) baking dish, creating an even layer. Layer the potatoes on top of the beef, overlapping them as needed and covering the entire surface of the dish. Repeat with the eggplant. Spoon the cooked onion and bell pepper over the eggplant and spread evenly. Pour the cooking liquid evenly over everything, then place the tomato slices on top, evenly spreading them out. The liquid level should come up just below the surface of the tomato layer.

7 Cover the dish tightly with aluminum foil and bake for 45 minutes. Uncover and bake for another 15 minutes, until the cooking liquid has slightly reduced.

8 Garnish with chopped parsley (if using) and serve with rice and salad.

Note

To make this dish vegetarian, skip the ground beef and follow the recipe as directed.

Lamb Maqluba
UPSIDE-DOWN RICE

YIELD: 6 to 8 servings

PREP TIME: 30 minutes

COOK TIME: 1 hour and 45 minutes

◇◇◇◇◇

LAMB AND BROTH

2 tablespoons vegetable oil

2 pounds (900 g) bone-in lamb shoulder, cut into 2- to 3-inch (5 to 7.5 cm) pieces (see Note on page 182)

2 cinnamon sticks

5 green cardamom pods

6 whole allspice berries

6 whole cloves

3 bay leaves

3½ teaspoons kosher salt, divided

½ teaspoon turmeric

1 teaspoon black pepper

¼ cup (60 g) tomato paste

MAQLUBA

4 Italian eggplants (2⅔ pounds, or 1.2 kg), ends trimmed, peeled lengthwise every other stripe, in a zebra pattern, and cut into ¾-inch-thick (2 cm) rounds

2 large yellow potatoes, peeled and cut into ½-inch-thick (13 mm) rounds

½ cup (120 ml) plus 3 tablespoons olive oil, divided

1 teaspoon kosher salt, divided

2 small yellow onions, sliced ¼ inch (6 mm) thick

1 medium red bell pepper, seeds removed and sliced ½ inch (13 mm) thick

½ teaspoon black pepper

Maqluba is a dish that you can make for guests and sort of sell like a "dinner and a show" type of evening, because flipping the maqluba pot is so much fun, especially with a crowd around cheering you on. We grew up on my mom's delicious maqluba, a dish made across Iraq, but it is also known in Palestine, Syria, and other neighboring countries. The Iraqi version is slightly different than the Levantine one, but I've never had a maqluba I didn't love. Every version is delicious, simply because of the technique—layers of meat (chicken or lamb) and vegetables underneath a bed of rice, left to simmer together for a while. The flavors all infuse, resulting in the most delicious rice dish you'll ever taste.

1 TO MAKE THE LAMB AND BROTH: In a pressure cooker or large pot, heat the vegetable oil over medium heat for 1 minute. Add the lamb pieces and sear for 2 to 3 minutes on each side, until lightly golden, working in batches to avoid overcrowding. Add 3 cups (720 ml) of water, the cinnamon sticks, cardamom pods, allspice berries, cloves, bay leaves, and 1 teaspoon of the salt. If using a pressure cooker, pressure-cook on high for 25 minutes; if using the stovetop, cover with the lid and boil over medium heat for 40 to 60 minutes, until the lamb is tender.

2 Once the lamb is cooked, transfer it to a plate. Strain the broth from the whole spices and pour it into a large bowl or a 6-cup (1.4 L) measuring cup. Add the turmeric, remaining 2½ teaspoons salt, 1 teaspoon black pepper, and tomato paste. Mix well to combine and add additional water to make 5½ cups (1.3 L) of liquid in total. Set aside.

3 MEANWHILE, MAKE THE MAQLUBA: Preheat the oven to 450°F (230°C). Line two large, rimmed sheet pans with parchment paper.

4 Lay the eggplant on one of the prepared sheet pans and the potatoes on the other. Toss with ¼ cup (60 ml) each of the olive oil and ¼ teaspoon each of the salt, then readjust the rounds into a single layer. Bake for 45 minutes, or until the eggplant and potatoes are golden brown and tender.

5 In a large skillet, heat the remaining 3 tablespoons olive oil over medium heat. Add the sliced onions and bell peppers and cook, stirring often, for 6 to 7 minutes, until both vegetables are softened. Season with the remaining ½ teaspoon salt and the ½ teaspoon black pepper. Transfer to a plate.

CONTINUED ▸

1 large tomato, sliced ½ inch (13 mm) thick

18 ounces (510 g) canned chickpeas, drained and rinsed

2½ cups (500 g) long-grain white basmati rice, rinsed until the water runs clear and drained completely

FOR GARNISHING AND SERVING

2 teaspoons olive oil (optional)

¼ cup (30 g) slivered almonds (optional)

¼ cup (13 g) finely chopped fresh parsley

Plain, whole-milk yogurt

Salata (page 44)

Note

To make with chicken, follow the recipe as directed using 2 pounds (900 g) of bone-in chicken leg quarters but reduce the cook time of the chicken to 15 minutes if using a pressure cooker and 30 minutes if using a stove. To make it vegetarian, omit the meat and place 6 cups (1.4 L) of vegetable broth in a large saucepan with the cinnamon, cardamom, allspice, bay leaves, cloves, tomato paste, and turmeric. Add 2½ teaspoons of kosher salt and let simmer over medium heat, covered, for 20 minutes. Strain the broth and continue the recipe at step 3.

6 In a large 5.5 quart (5.2 L) nonstick pot, first make a layer of the tomato slices, followed by a layer of the eggplant. You will have enough eggplant to make 2 or 3 layers; simply lay the pieces on top of each other. Next, layer the potatoes, then the lamb pieces. Spoon the onions and bell pepper on top and place the chickpeas around the lamb to create an even layer. Finally, add the rice and flatten it down using a spoon.

7 Gently pour the broth on top of the rice; the liquid should just barely cover the surface of the rice.

8 Cover the pot with the lid and place it on the stovetop over high heat for 5 to 7 minutes. Once the maqluba looks like it is heated with steam and has slight bubbles on the surface, cover it again, and reduce the heat to medium-low and let cook for 20 minutes.

9 After 20 minutes, uncover the pot and very gently stir only the topmost layer of rice. The goal is to move the topmost layer of rice, which will look dry and uncooked, slightly underneath, and bring the cooked rice to the top; this will rotate the rice to give all of it a chance to cook evenly without the addition of more liquid (more liquid will make the rice too mushy). Cover the pot again and let cook for another 30 minutes. Remove the lid and check the rice for doneness; all the grains should be soft and fluffy. Turn off the heat, place the lid back on, and let sit for 10 minutes.

10 TO MAKE THE GARNISH: If using, in a small skillet, heat the 2 teaspoons olive oil over medium heat for 1 minute. Add the almonds and toast for 4 to 5 minutes, until golden, stirring continuously.

11 To serve, use a large, round, flat serving tray. Remove the lid and place the serving tray upside down, covering the pot like a lid. Grab the handles of the pot, at the same time gripping the edges of the tray, and gently but swiftly flip the pot upside down. Allow the flipped pot to stay in place over the tray for 5 to 10 minutes to help gravity slowly bring the maqluba down and hold its shape. Slowly remove the pot to reveal the maqluba. If there are some vegetables stuck to the bottom of the pan, gently spoon them on top.

12 Garnish with the toasted almonds (if using) and chopped parsley and serve with yogurt and salad.

Moroccan Lamb Tagine with Jeweled Couscous

YIELD: 4 to 6 servings

PREP TIME: 15 minutes

COOK TIME: 2 hours and 15 minutes

◇◇◇◇◇

TAGINE

2¼ pounds (1 kg) bone-in lamb shoulder, cut into 2-inch (5 cm) pieces

2 teaspoons kosher salt, divided, plus more to taste

1 teaspoon black pepper

2 tablespoons vegetable oil, plus more if needed

2 large onions, finely chopped

6 large cloves garlic, crushed

1½ teaspoons ground cumin

½ teaspoon ground turmeric

1 teaspoon paprika

½ teaspoon ground cinnamon

½ teaspoon ground coriander

½ teaspoon ground ginger

2 cups (480 ml) chicken or vegetable broth

4 large carrots, cut into ½-inch-thick (13 mm) rounds

2 large yellow potatoes, cut into 1-inch (2.5 cm) cubes

1½ cups (195 g) pitted prunes (optional)

COUSCOUS

1½ cups (360 ml) chicken or vegetable broth

½ teaspoon kosher salt, plus more if needed

2 tablespoons olive oil

1 cup (195 g) dried couscous

½ cup pine nuts (60 g) or slivered almonds (70 g)

1 cup (188 g) pomegranate arils

Tagine refers to both a common North African cone-shaped cooking vessel made of clay and also the slow-cooked savory stew that is cooked in it. The clay tagine is designed to contain the steam inside the vessel, keeping the stew moist as it slowly cooks for hours. You can easily replicate this technique using a heavy cast-iron Dutch oven.

1 **TO MAKE THE TAGINE:** Preheat the oven to 325°F (165°C). Season the lamb on all sides with 1½ teaspoons of the salt and the pepper.

2 In a large oven-safe pot or Dutch oven, heat the vegetable oil over medium-high heat. Add the lamb, working in batches to avoid overcrowding, and sear for a few minutes per side, or until browned. Transfer to a plate.

3 Add the onions to the same pot and cook for 4 to 5 minutes, stirring often, until softened (add more oil if necessary). Add the garlic, cumin, turmeric, paprika, cinnamon, coriander, and ginger and cook, stirring constantly, for a few minutes until fragrant. Add the 2 cups (480 ml) broth and place the lamb back into the pot. Cover with the lid and bring to a boil over medium heat. Once boiling, carefully transfer the pot to the oven and bake, covered, for 1 hour and 15 minutes.

4 After the stew has baked for 1 hour and 15 minutes, remove from the oven. Sprinkle the carrots and potatoes with the remaining ½ teaspoon salt, then add them and the prunes to the pot, submerging them in the liquid as best as possible. Cover and bake for 45 more minutes, or until the meat is tender and falling off the bone. If there is too much liquid, let simmer on the stovetop over medium heat, uncovered, to reduce it slightly.

5 **MEANWHILE, MAKE THE COUSCOUS:** In a medium saucepan over medium-high heat, bring the 1½ cups (360 ml) broth to a boil and season with the ½ teaspoon salt. Add the olive oil. Place the couscous in a large bowl. Pour the boiling broth over the couscous, mix well, and cover with a tight-fitting lid or aluminum foil. Let the couscous steam for 5 to 7 minutes.

6 Add the nuts to a small skillet and toast them for a few minutes, or until golden and fragrant, stirring continuously.

7 Uncover the couscous and fluff with a fork. Taste and adjust for salt if necessary. Mix in the pomegranate arils and toasted nuts. Serve the tagine with the couscous on the side.

Slow-Roasted Leg of Lamb

YIELD: 6 to 8 servings

PREP TIME: 10 minutes

COOK TIME: 5 hours

◇◇◇◇◇

SPICE PASTE

1½ teaspoons ground coriander

1½ teaspoons ground cumin

½ teaspoon ground cloves

½ teaspoon ground cinnamon

½ teaspoon ground cardamom

2 tablespoons olive oil

Juice of ½ lemon

LEG OF LAMB

4½ teaspoons kosher salt (use ¾ teaspoon per pound; adjust accordingly to size of leg)

6 pounds (2.7 kg) bone-in leg of lamb, brought to room temperature 1 hour before baking and fat trimmed (see Notes on page 188 for adjustments based on size of leg)

10 large cloves garlic, peeled

3 large yellow onions, cut in half

FOR GARNISHING AND SERVING

Pomegranate arils

Fresh mint leaves

Moroccan Chermoula (page 26) (optional)

Roz Asfar (page 71; see Notes on page 188) (optional)

When it comes to hospitality, Arabs are well known for being masters of the art. Ensuring guests are welcomed and honored in Arab households is an ancient practice—almost a ritual. And because lamb is one of the most expensive meats, serving it as the centerpiece of a dinner table is common when inviting friends and family to share a meal. Growing up, I watched my mom labor over huge spreads of food for large parties, and every single one of her menus had a lamb dish. This slow-roasted leg of lamb is my go-to dish when I am entertaining, simply because it is impressive yet requires hardly any effort on my part. The right seasoning mix, the right roasting technique, and a good quality leg of lamb are all it takes for my oven to do the work for me.

1 Preheat the oven to 350°F (175°C).

2 TO MAKE THE SPICE PASTE: In a small bowl, mix the coriander, cumin, cloves, cinnamon, cardamom, oil and lemon juice until a thick paste forms.

3 TO MAKE THE LEG OF LAMB: On a large cutting board or work surface, rub the salt all over the lamb leg, ensuring you cover the full surface area, then repeat with the spice paste.

4 Using a sharp knife, make 8 to 10 large slits in the side of the lamb facing up, at least 1½ inches (4 cm) deep. Insert the garlic cloves inside the slits; you may need to cut some of the cloves in half if they are too big. At this point, you can either cover the lamb leg and let it marinate for 2 hours or overnight in the refrigerator, or you can proceed with the recipe.

5 Place the onion halves on the bottom of a large roasting dish that fits the lamb leg, then place the seasoned lamb on top. Pour 3 cups (720 ml) of water into the bottom of the roasting dish. Use a large piece of parchment paper to cover the lamb well and try to seal in all the sides as best as you can; it is fine if the parchment paper touches the water. Use aluminum foil to cover the whole roasting dish well, securing all the edges tightly; use 2 layers of overlapping pieces of foil to ensure a very tight seal.

CONTINUED ▶

6 Bake for 4 to 5 hours, until the lamb is fork-tender and falling off the bone, checking the lamb for doneness after 3 hours. Let rest, covered, for 30 minutes.

7 Garnish with pomegranate arils and mint leaves and serve over a bed of roz asfar with almonds and raisins (if using) and chermoula (if using) on the side for topping.

Notes

+ If your lamb leg is 4 to 5 pounds (1.8 to 2.3 kg), decrease the cooking time to 3 to 4 hours. Check the lamb leg at the 3-hour mark and add time if required. Ensure you adjust the amount of salt used if you use a smaller lamb leg.

+ If you are cooking roz asfar to go along with the lamb, remove the roasting dish from the oven at the 3-hour mark. Carefully tilt the roasting dish and use a ladle to scoop out all the liquid. Use this liquid as broth for cooking your rice, then replenish the lamb with 1 cup (240 ml) of water, reseal it, and return it to the oven for another 1 to 2 hours.

Egyptian Koshari
LENTILS, RICE & PASTA

YIELD: 6 servings

PREP TIME: 10 minutes

COOK TIME: 1 hour and 30 minutes

◇◇◇◇◇

CRISPY ONIONS

4 large yellow onions, cut in half and
thinly sliced into half-moons (use
a sharp knife, a mandolin slicer,
or a food processor with the slicer
attachment)

2 tablespoons all-purpose flour

2 tablespoons cornstarch

Vegetable oil

¼ teaspoon kosher salt

LENTILS AND RICE

1 large onion, finely chopped

2 cloves garlic, minced

1 cup (200 g) brown lentils, rinsed
and drained

3 cups (720 ml) chicken broth,
divided

2 cups (380 g) Calrose rice (or any
medium-grain rice), rinsed until
the water runs clear and drained
completely

1½ teaspoons kosher salt

PASTA

7 ounces (200 g) elbow or ditalini
pasta

2 teaspoons kosher salt

Koshari is Egypt's national dish. And when I explain the components, you may be a bit perplexed, as I was when I first learned about it. How can one recipe have so many carbs? But once you get a taste, it will all make sense. This humble dish became widespread across Egypt due to its affordability. It combines lentils, rice, pasta, and chickpeas. The real magic happens when they are topped with a garlicky, tangy tomato sauce and then smothered with sweet and crispy fried onions. The oil that the onions are fried in is used to cook the other components, adding further flavor and depth. It is quite addictive! It's also typically served with a side of dukkah, which in this case is a white vinegar sauce flavored with garlic, coriander, and cumin (as opposed to the nut, seed, and spice mix on page 33). Most Egyptians also serve it with a spicier tomato sauce on the side for those who love additional heat. Although this dish has many components, it's quite simple to make and truly unique. My obsession with koshari began when I had a taste of it at a local Egyptian restaurant. After that, it became a regular dish that I make at home, perfecting it over the years.

1 TO MAKE THE CRISPY ONIONS: In a large bowl, combine the sliced onions with the flour and cornstarch and lightly coat them.

2 In a large skillet, heat enough oil over medium-high heat (at least ¾ cup, or 180 ml) to cover the onions. Add the onions so that they are immersed in the oil and not overcrowded, working in two batches, and cook until the edges start to turn golden. Gently bring the outer ones to the center and continue frying until they all turn golden brown; be careful not to burn them. With a slotted spoon, remove the onions to a paper towel–lined tray to absorb the excess oil. Sprinkle with the ¼ teaspoon salt.

3 Strain the remaining onion oil in the pan through a fine-mesh strainer and reserve.

4 TO MAKE THE LENTILS AND RICE: In a large pot, heat ½ cup (120 ml) of the reserved onion oil over medium heat. Add the chopped onion and cook, stirring often, until softened and translucent, 5 to 7 minutes. Add the 2 minced garlic cloves and cook, stirring constantly, for 1 minute.

CONTINUED ▶

DUKKAH (VINEGAR SAUCE)

3 cloves garlic, minced

½ cup (120 ml) white vinegar

2 teaspoons ground coriander

½ teaspoon ground cumin

½ teaspoon kosher salt

½ teaspoon chili flakes

Juice of ½ small lemon

TOMATO SAUCE

7 cloves garlic, minced

¼ cup (60 ml) white vinegar

2 teaspoons ground coriander

1 teaspoon ground cumin

½ teaspoon chili flakes

½ teaspoon kosher salt

½ teaspoon black pepper

2½ cups (600 ml) tomato passata
   (puree)

CHICKPEAS

18 ounces (510 g) canned chickpeas,
   drained and rinsed

½ teaspoon ground cumin

⅛ teaspoon kosher salt

Note

Koshari can be served layered in one large platter, or each component can be served in a separate dish for guests to create their own combinations.

5 Add the lentils to the pot along with 2 cups (480 ml) of the broth. Bring to a boil, then cover with the lid, reduce the heat to low, and let cook for 10 to 15 minutes, until the liquid has mostly disappeared.

6 Add the rice to the pot along with the remaining 1 cup (240 ml) broth and the 1½ teaspoons salt. Increase the heat to medium-high and bring to a boil. Cover with the lid, reduce the heat to low, and let cook for 20 minutes, undisturbed. Add 1 tablespoon of the reserved onion oil and gently mix it in.

7 MEANWHILE, MAKE THE PASTA: Fill a medium saucepan halfway with water, add the 2 teaspoons salt, and bring to a boil. Add the pasta and cook according to the package instructions for al dente. Drain.

8 TO MAKE THE DUKKAH: Add 1 tablespoon of the reserved onion oil and the 3 minced garlic cloves to a medium saucepan over medium heat. Cook, stirring constantly, for a few minutes, or until lightly golden and fragrant. Add the ½ cup (120 ml) vinegar, the coriander, ½ teaspoon cumin, ½ teaspoon salt, and chili flakes and stir together for a few seconds. Remove from the heat. Add the lemon juice and transfer to a small serving bowl.

9 TO MAKE THE TOMATO SAUCE: In the same pot the dukkah was cooked in, add 2 tablespoons of the reserved onion oil and the 7 minced garlic cloves over medium heat, cooking, stirring often, until the garlic is lightly golden and fragrant. Add the ¼ cup (60 ml) vinegar, coriander, 1 teaspoon cumin, chili flakes, ½ teaspoon salt, pepper, and passata. Stir the sauce for a few seconds, then simmer over medium-low for 5 to 7 minutes to thicken, stirring occasionally.

10 TO MAKE THE CHICKPEAS: Add the chickpeas to a small bowl with 1 tablespoon of the reserved onion oil, the ½ teaspoon cumin, and ⅛ teaspoon salt. Toss together.

11 Spoon the lentils and rice onto a large platter, followed by a layer of pasta and then the chickpeas (see Note). Spoon some of the tomato sauce on top, then garnish with the crispy onions. Serve the dukkah and remaining tomato sauce on the side.

Main Dishes Soups & Stews

Fasolia Yabsa

WHITE BEAN STEW

YIELD: 6 to 8 servings
PREP TIME: 10 minutes
COOK TIME: 2 hours

◇◇◇◇◇

18 ounces (500 g) bone-in lamb or
    veal shoulder pieces, cut into 2-inch
    (5 cm) pieces (see Notes)
2¼ teaspoons kosher salt, divided,
    plus more if needed
½ teaspoon black pepper, divided,
    plus more if needed
2 tablespoons olive oil
2 large onions, finely chopped
5 tablespoons tomato paste
2 cups (360 g) dried white kidney
    beans (see Notes), soaked
    overnight and drained

FOR SERVING
Roz Bi Shaariya (page 67)
Salata (page 44)

Notes

+ It is easiest if you ask the
  butcher to cut the bone-in
  meat into smaller pieces.

+ You can use 38 ounces
  (1.1 kg) of canned beans,
  drained and rinsed, instead
  of dried ones. Follow the
  instructions, but do not add
  the canned beans until later
  in step 4; after the veal has
  cooked for 1 hour and is
  fully tender, add the beans
  and cook for 20 to 30 more
  minutes.

My favorite memory from my childhood is walking home from school, excited to open the door and smell what was for dinner that day. It was usually stew with rice, because that's typical Arab home cooking. But I enjoyed guessing which type of stew it was based on the aroma I was hit with when I walked in. It was a happy day if it was fasolia yabsa! This is the stew most known across Iraq, especially when made from dried beans and bone-in lamb and scooped over a bowl of Roz Bi Shaariya (page 67)—my definition of the ultimate comfort food. I do, however, often take the shortcut of using canned beans; they really do get the job done, and I am not one to judge!

1 Season the meat pieces with ½ teaspoon of the salt and ¼ teaspoon of the pepper.

2 In a large pot, heat the oil over medium heat. Add the meat and sear for 5 to 6 minutes, flipping until all sides are lightly browned.

3 Add the onions and ½ teaspoon of the salt and cook, stirring often, for 5 minutes, until softened. Stir in the tomato paste and continue to cook for 2 to 3 minutes.

4 Add the drained beans along with 5½ cups (1.3 L) of water, the remaining 1¼ teaspoons salt, and the remaining ¼ teaspoon pepper. Mix everything together. Increase the heat to high and bring to a boil, then reduce the heat to medium and cook for 1 to 1½ hours, until the veal and beans are tender. You may need to replenish the water as the level goes down; check every 20 minutes or so to adjust (the water should be enough to cover the beans and meat). Taste and adjust for salt and pepper if necessary. The stew will thicken slightly due to the beans but should still have enough liquid.

5 Ladle into bowls and serve with rice and salad.

Margat Batata
CURRIED POTATO STEW

YIELD: 6 servings

PREP TIME: 15 minutes

COOK TIME: 1 hour and 10 minutes

◇◇◇◇◇

2 tablespoons olive oil

1⅓ pounds (600 g) bone-in veal or lamb shoulder, cut into 2-inch (5 cm) pieces (see Note)

3 large bay leaves

3 teaspoons kosher salt, divided

7 medium yellow potatoes, peeled

2 teaspoons curry powder

3 medium onions, peeled

¼ teaspoon black pepper, plus more if needed

½ cup plus 2 tablespoons (150 g) tomato paste, plus more to taste

2 tablespoons pomegranate molasses

Roz Bi Shaariya (page 67), for serving

This stew was one of my dad's favorites, so my mom made it often. Nowadays, it's my husband's favorite, so I also make it often. As I grew older, I was perplexed by the idea of scooping a carb-heavy stew on top of more carbs in the form of rice, but it just works, and it's the perfect winter meal. The curry powder is what gives this stew its unique flavor, bringing to life all the other simple ingredients. You can make this stew with veal or lamb, but I recommend both cuts be bone-in, because the bones develop a lot of the flavor of the stew.

1 In a large pot, heat the oil over medium heat. Add the meat pieces and brown for 2 minutes per side on all sides, or until lightly seared.

2 Cover the meat with water, add the bay leaves and 1 teaspoon of the salt, and bring to a boil over medium-high heat, skimming any scum that floats to the surface and discarding it. Let boil for 40 to 50 minutes, half-covered with the lid, until the meat is tender.

3 Meanwhile, cut the potatoes in half, then cut each half in half again.

4 Add the potato pieces and curry powder and continue to cook at a rolling boil for 10 minutes, replenishing the water as needed so that it is covering the meat and potatoes.

5 Add the onions, 1½ teaspoons of the salt, the pepper, tomato paste, and pomegranate molasses. Ensure the water level is covering the veal and vegetables and continue to cook at a rolling boil for another 15 to 20 minutes. Check the potatoes for doneness; they should be soft but still holding their shape. Taste and add the remaining ½ teaspoon salt if necessary. Add more pepper if necessary. The final consistency of the stew should be a thick liquid.

6 Ladle into bowls and serve with rice.

Note
It is easiest if you ask the butcher to cut the bone-in meat into smaller pieces.

Margat Bamya
OKRA STEW

YIELD: 6 servings
PREP TIME: 10 minutes
COOK TIME: 1 hour

◇◇◇◇◇

1½ pounds (650 g) bone-in veal (see Notes), cut into 2-inch (5 cm) pieces

2 teaspoons kosher salt, divided, plus more if needed

½ teaspoon black pepper, plus more if needed

3 tablespoons olive oil

1 large onion, finely chopped

6 tablespoons tomato paste

28 ounces (800 g) frozen small okra (see Notes)

8 large cloves garlic, roughly chopped

1½ tablespoons pomegranate molasses

Bamya means "okra" in Arabic, and it's usually cooked in a tomato-based stew until the okra is soft and melts in your mouth. It's a stew that I personally loved growing up, but I came to realize as an adult that many of my friends did not enjoy eating it because of the subtle sliminess okra can give off. But when okra is cooked right, there should not be any sliminess. The trick is to ensure it is not cut up before cooking; my mom would only trim the tops very slightly and leave it whole. I may be biased, but I think my family's Iraqi-style okra stew is the most delicious because of the excessive use of two things: garlic, which complements the okra, and pomegranate molasses.

1 Season the veal pieces with ½ teaspoon of the salt and the pepper.

2 In a large pot over medium heat, add the oil, onion, and ½ teaspoon of the salt and cook, stirring often, for 5 to 6 minutes, until the onion is softened and translucent. Add the veal and sear for 5 to 6 minutes, flipping until all sides are lightly browned. Stir in the tomato paste and continue to cook for another few minutes. Add the okra, garlic, pomegranate molasses, remaining 1 teaspoon salt, and about 6 cups (1.4 L) of water to the pot and mix everything well. Bring to a rolling boil over medium heat, then boil for about 30 minutes with the pot half-covered with the lid.

3 After 30 minutes, check the tenderness of the okra and the meat and taste and adjust the salt and pepper if necessary. If the okra and meat are both still slightly firm, add more water (2 to 3 cups, or 480 to 720 ml) and continue boiling for another 30 minutes; if they are both tender, turn off the heat and serve.

Notes

+ Use good-quality veal or lamb as they are typically more tender than beef; however, if all you have on hand is bone-in beef, it will work, but you may need to pre-boil it first.

+ It is easiest if you ask the butcher to cut the bone-in veal into smaller pieces.

+ Small or young okra is recommended as it is much more tender than larger okra.

Iraqi Tashreeb
BEEF & CHICKPEA STEW OVER BREAD

YIELD: 6 to 8 servings
PREP TIME: 10 minutes
COOK TIME: 3 hours

◇◇◇◇◇

4½ pounds (2 kg) veal shanks
 (4 large pieces; see Notes)
4 teaspoons kosher salt, divided,
 plus more if necessary
½ teaspoon black pepper
5 dried limes, soaked in boiling water
 for 5 minutes
2 tablespoons avocado oil
4 medium yellow onions, cut into
 eighths
5 green cardamom pods
3 bay leaves
¾ cup (180 g) tomato paste
18 ounces (510 g) canned chickpeas,
 drained and rinsed

FOR SERVING

3 large loaves Iraqi or lavash bread
 (or substitute thick Greek-style
 pita bread)
Finely chopped fresh parsley
Whole green onions, trimmed
Sliced sweet white onions

Notes

+ You can also use bone-in
 lamb shoulder cut into
 medium-size pieces.

+ To cook using a pressure
 cooker, at step 5, pressure-
 cook on high for 25 minutes.
 Release the pressure, then
 add the chickpeas.

Iraqi cuisine is known to be quite meat-heavy—we savor and enjoy the umami from stewing bone-in meat, and this dish celebrates exactly that. Growing up, I used to always hear my meat-loving uncles say that if you did not have red meat and savor the bones, then you did not eat meat at all. *Tashreeb* is an Arabic word that means "to soak," which is how this dish is served. Large loaves of thick Iraqi bread resembling lavash are torn into pieces and placed in serving bowls. A tomato-based meat stew with onions and chickpeas is ladled on top. The bread soaks up the broth, resulting in the most delicious and hearty bowl. There are other versions of tashreeb that are made with chicken and some that do not add tomato to the broth.

1 Preheat the oven to 325°F (165°C).

2 Season the veal shanks on both sides with 1½ teaspoons of the salt and the pepper. Drain the dried limes and use a knife to make 2 or 3 slits in each one, to allow the flavor to be extracted.

3 In a large oven-safe pot or Dutch oven, heat the oil over medium heat. Add the shanks, working in batches, and sear them for 1 to 2 minutes per side, or until golden. Transfer to a plate.

4 In the same pot, add the onions along with ½ teaspoon of the salt and cook, stirring often, for 4 to 5 minutes, until lightly golden. Add the cardamom pods, bay leaves, and pierced limes and toast for 1 minute, stirring often. Add the tomato paste and cook while stirring for a few seconds. Add 5 cups (1.2 L) of water and the remaining 2 teaspoons salt.

5 Add the veal shanks back into the pot and bring to a boil. Once boiling, cover the pot with the lid and carefully place it in the oven. Braise the shanks for 3 hours, or until the meat is tender and falling off the bones. Check on them after 1½ hours to make sure the liquid level is adequate; there should be enough liquid to fill at least three-quarters of the pot. If required, add ½ to 1 cup (120 to 240 ml) of water. Add the chickpeas at the 1½-hour mark. After 3 hours, taste the broth and adjust for salt if necessary and check to ensure the veal is falling off the bones. Remove from the oven.

6 Tear up the bread into bite-size pieces and place as much as preferred in the serving bowls. Ladle the stew over the bread in each bowl. Serve with parsley and green and white onions.

Unstuffed Cabbage Soup

YIELD: 6 to 8 servings
PREP TIME: 15 minutes
COOK TIME: 50 minutes

◇◇◇◇◇

2 tablespoons olive oil

Cloves from 2 heads garlic, peeled and finely chopped

1 pound (450 g) lean ground beef

2½ teaspoons kosher salt, plus more if needed

1 teaspoon ground allspice

½ teaspoon ground cinnamon

¼ teaspoon black pepper

1 cup (240 g) tomato paste

½ large head green cabbage, roughly chopped (see Note)

6 cups (1.5 L) chicken or vegetable broth

⅓ cup (75 g) short-grain rice, rinsed until the water runs clear and drained completely

¼ cup (60 ml) fresh lemon juice

2 teaspoons dried mint

FOR GARNISHING AND SERVING

¼ cup (13 g) finely chopped fresh parsley

Dried mint

Lemon wedges

One of the most delicious stuffed dishes cooked across the region is stuffed cabbage. The cabbage is stuffed with a mixture of rice, ground beef, and copious amounts of garlic, then simmered in a lemony broth until the cabbage melts in your mouth. But stuffing and rolling leaf after leaf is a labor of love. This soup is how I replicate the flavors of stuffed cabbage but in a fraction of the time. It's hearty, vibrant, and nutritious, perfect for a cold winter night. Feel free to go wild with the garlic, lemon, and mint quantities—they are the magic trio!

1 In a large pot over medium heat, combine the oil and garlic and cook, stirring continuously, over medium heat for 1 to 2 minutes, until the garlic is fragrant and slightly golden.

2 Add the ground beef and cook, breaking it up into small pieces with a wooden spoon, for 6 to 7 minutes, until browned.

3 Add the salt, allspice, cinnamon, pepper, and tomato paste, mix everything together, and cook for another 1 to 2 minutes. Add the cabbage and stir to combine.

4 Add the broth and stir to combine. Cover with the lid and let simmer over medium heat for 30 minutes.

5 Add the rice, stir, and continue to cook, covered, for 10 minutes. Uncover the pot and add the lemon juice and mint. Stir to combine and taste and adjust the salt if necessary. If the soup is too thick, add a bit of water to thin it out to desired consistency.

6 Ladle into bowls and garnish with the parsley and mint and serve with lemon wedges for squeezing.

Note

To chop the cabbage, start by slicing the cabbage down the middle, splitting it into 2 equal halves. Place each half, cut side down, and slice down the middle to create 4 equal quarters. Cut off the core and stem from each quarter and discard, then place each quarter flat side down and slice into squares.

Shorbat Lsan El Asfoor
MEATBALL & ORZO SOUP

YIELD: 4 to 6 servings
PREP TIME: 10 minutes
COOK TIME: 50 minutes

◇◇◇◇◇

MEATBALLS

⅔ pound (300 g) lean ground beef
½ teaspoon kosher salt
¼ teaspoon black pepper
½ teaspoon seven spice
1 teaspoon onion powder
1 teaspoon garlic powder
1 teaspoon paprika
3 tablespoons bread crumbs
2 tablespoons olive oil

SOUP

2 tablespoons olive oil
1 medium yellow onion, finely chopped
1 teaspoon kosher salt, plus more if needed
2 large cloves garlic, crushed
½ cup (120 g) tomato paste
5 cups (1.2 L) chicken broth
2½ ounces (70 g) orzo

FOR GARNISHING AND SERVING

¼ cup (13 g) finely chopped fresh parsley
Pita bread

Whenever I make kofta or meatballs, I always make sure to keep some in the fridge to make this soup the next day. Orzo is called *lsan el asfour* in Arabic, which translates to "bird's tongue," after the pasta shape. I remember how fun I used to think it was to pretend to be eating birds' tongues when I was little. I make the meatballs for this soup extra small, because somehow they are more satisfying to eat that way in one bite, along with the orzo. This is my kids' favorite soup.

1 TO MAKE THE MEATBALLS: In a medium bowl, combine all the meatball ingredients beef, salt, pepper, seven spice, onion and garlic powders, paprika, and bread crumbs and mix well using your hands. Roll into ½-inch (13 mm) meatballs.

2 In a medium pot, heat the oil over medium heat. Add the meatballs, working in batches, and sear for 2 to 3 minutes, until golden on most sides. Transfer to a plate.

3 TO MAKE THE SOUP: In the same pot, add the oil, onion, and salt and cook, stirring often, for 5 to 6 minutes, until softened and translucent. Add the garlic and cook, stirring often, for a few minutes, or until fragrant. Add the tomato paste and stir for a few seconds.

4 Pour in the broth and add the meatballs back into the pot. Cover the pot with the lid and bring to a boil over high heat. Once boiling, reduce the heat to medium and let simmer, covered, for 20 minutes.

5 Remove the lid and add the orzo. Stir well, then cover and let cook for 15 minutes. Taste and adjust the soup for salt if necessary. Check the orzo to ensure it is cooked to al dente, or softer if desired.

6 Ladle into bowls, garnish with chopped parsley, and serve with pita bread.

Turkish Chicken Noodle Soup

YIELD: 4 to 6 servings
PREP TIME: 10 minutes
COOK TIME: 45 minutes

◇◇◇◇◇

2 tablespoons olive oil

1 tablespoon unsalted butter

1 large yellow onion, finely chopped

2 teaspoons kosher salt, divided, plus
   more if needed

4 large cloves garlic, crushed

5½ ounces (160 g) carrots, shredded

2 teaspoons paprika

½ teaspoon black pepper

3 tablespoons all-purpose flour

8 cups (2 L) chicken broth

3½ cups (685 g) shredded cooked
   chicken (see Note)

5⅓ ounces (150 g) pasta shape of
   choice (such as gemelli, fusilli, or
   cavatappi)

FOR GARNISHING AND SERVING

¼ cup (13 g) finely chopped fresh
   parsley

Lemon wedges

Every culture has their own chicken noodle soup, and this Turkish version is the one I love. My mom always made us a simple vermicelli noodle soup with a tomato broth, and we devoured it. This soup reminds me of hers but with a bit more flair and body, using onions, carrots, spices, and a bit of flour to thicken everything. The flavor is made even better the longer you simmer the soup.

1 In a large pot, heat the oil and butter over medium heat. Once the butter has melted, add the onion and 1 teaspoon of the salt and cook, stirring often, for 6 to 7 minutes, until the onion has softened and is lightly golden.

2 Add the garlic, carrots, paprika, and pepper and continue to cook for 3 to 4 minutes. Add the flour and stir for 30 seconds until incorporated with the vegetables and seasonings.

3 Add the broth and bring the soup to a boil over high heat. Once boiling, cover the pot with the lid, reduce the heat to medium, and let simmer for 20 minutes.

4 Remove the lid and add the shredded chicken and pasta, along with the remaining 1 teaspoon salt. Stir everything together, then let simmer, covered, for another 15 to 20 minutes, until the pasta is cooked. Taste and adjust for salt if necessary.

5 Ladle into bowls, garnish with parsley, and serve with lemon wedges for squeezing.

Note

If you do not have pre-shredded rotisserie chicken, you can make it along with the homemade chicken stock. In a large pot, heat 2 tablespoons of olive oil over medium heat for 1 minute. Sear 1½ pounds (700 g) of bone-in chicken thighs, drumsticks, or leg quarters for 2 to 3 minutes on each side, until lightly golden. Add 1 quartered yellow onion, with 2 large carrots and 1 celery rib, all roughly chopped. Add 2 teaspoons kosher salt, 2 bay leaves, 4 green cardamom pods, and 1 cinnamon stick and enough water to cover the chicken and bring to a boil. Reduce the heat to medium-low and let simmer for 1 hour (or up to 3 hours). Turn off the heat, remove the chicken, and shred it with a fork. Strain the broth and use it in this recipe.

Margat Sabanikh
SPINACH & CHICKPEA STEW

YIELD: 6 to 8 servings

PREP TIME: 10 minutes

COOK TIME: 40 minutes

◇◇◇◇◇

¼ cup (60 ml) olive oil

2 medium yellow onions, diced

2 small bunches fresh dill, large stems removed and finely chopped

6 tablespoons tomato paste

2 teaspoons kosher salt, plus more if needed

½ teaspoon black pepper, plus more if needed

28 ounces (800 g) frozen chopped spinach, thawed for 5 minutes

3 dried limes, soaked in boiling water for 5 minutes

18 ounces (510 g) canned chickpeas, drained and rinsed

FOR SERVING

Pita bread

Roz Bi Shaariya (page 67)

This was one of my favorite stews growing up, but my mom would always make it with ground beef. I learned this vegetarian version from my sister, and it is perfect when I want to cook a vegetarian meal. It uses plenty of fresh dill and whole dried limes for a deep, earthy flavor. You don't miss out on the meat: the onions, spinach, chickpeas, and dill all simmer together as the stew thickens and the flavors balance out. I serve it over rice for the family, but I also love having it as a soup.

1 In a medium pot, heat the oil over medium heat. Add the onions and cook, stirring often, until softened and lightly browned, 6 to 7 minutes.

2 Add the dill and tomato paste and cook, stirring often, for 2 to 3 minutes. Add the salt, pepper, and spinach. Add enough water to cover the ingredients (4¼ to 6 ½ cups, or 1 to 1.5 L), filling the pot about halfway.

3 Drain the dried limes and use a knife to carefully make 2 or 3 slits in each one to allow the flavor to be extracted. Add them to the pot along with the chickpeas and bring to a boil. Cover the pot with the lid, reduce the heat to medium-low and let simmer for 20 minutes.

4 Uncover and let simmer for another 20 to 30 minutes, until the stew has thickened. (Simmer longer if you prefer it thicker, or less if you prefer a soup consistency.) Taste and adjust the salt and pepper if necessary.

5 Ladle into bowls and serve with pita bread and rice.

Shorbat Adas

LENTIL SOUP

YIELD: 8 servings
PREP TIME: 10 minutes
COOK TIME: 40 minutes

◇◇◇◇◇

3 tablespoons vegetable oil

2 large yellow onions, roughly chopped

1 large potato, peeled and roughly chopped

1 large carrot, peeled and roughly chopped

1½ teaspoons kosher salt, plus more if needed

1½ teaspoons ground cumin

½ teaspoon black pepper, or to taste

2 cups (370 g) split red lentils, rinsed and drained

8 cups (2 L) chicken broth or water, plus more if needed

FOR SERVING

Lemon wedges

Crunchy pita chips (see Note; optional)

While many Middle Eastern countries have their own unique soups, this lentil soup is the most universal. It is typically consumed every day during Ramadan, right when we break our fast. It's nutrient-dense and helps prime our bodies for food after a long day of fasting. This is the soup that I make regularly at my home simply because it requires very few ingredients, cooks quickly, and delivers on flavor. You'll find bags of it in my freezer as a core element of my emergency stash. You can add vegetables to it or make it with just onions. My mom always adds cumin and likes to keep the soup unblended. I like a smooth texture, so I blitz it with an immersion blender right before serving. Sometimes, to make it more special, I top it with crispy pita chips, which my kids love.

1 In a large pot, heat the oil over medium-high heat. Add the onions, potato, and carrot and cook, stirring often, for 4 to 5 minutes, until the vegetables are slightly browned. Add the salt, cumin, and pepper, stir, and cook for another 3 to 4 minutes.

2 Add the lentils and 8 cups (2 L) broth and mix well. Cover the pot with the lid and bring to a rolling boil. Reduce the heat to medium and let the soup cook, covered, for 30 to 45 minutes, until the vegetables and lentils are soft. Taste and adjust the salt if necessary. If you like the soup thinner, add more broth and let it cook for a few more minutes.

3 Turn off the heat and carefully blend the soup using an immersion blender right in the pot. (If you do not have an immersion blender, carefully transfer to a regular blender, blending in batches, until the consistency is smooth.)

4 Ladle into bowls and serve with lemon wedges for squeezing and crunchy pita chips (if using) for topping.

Note

To make the crunchy pita chips for topping, simply cut the desired amount of pita bread into small squares. Heat 2 to 3 tablespoons of olive oil in a skillet and fry the pita squares until golden and crunchy, stirring often.

Persian Ash Reshteh
HERBY NOODLE SOUP

YIELD: 6 to 8 servings
PREP TIME: 10 minutes
COOK TIME: 1 hour

◇◇◇◇◇

¼ cup (60 ml) olive oil

2 medium yellow onions, thinly sliced

3 teaspoons kosher salt, divided, plus more if needed

4 large cloves garlic, thinly sliced

3 teaspoons dried mint

1½ teaspoons ground turmeric

18 ounces (510 g) canned chickpeas, drained and rinsed

18 ounces (510 g) canned kidney beans, drained and rinsed

1 cup (200 g) green lentils, rinsed and drained

5 ounces (140 g) spaghetti or bucatini pasta

1½ cups (45 g) finely chopped fresh dill, thick stems removed

1 cup (60 g) finely chopped fresh parsley

1 cup (60 g) finely chopped fresh cilantro

2 cups (60 g) roughly chopped spinach

Juice of ½ lemon, plus more if needed

FOR GARNISHING AND SERVING

3 tablespoons olive oil

3 teaspoons dried mint

1 cup (240 ml) sour cream or Greek yogurt

I love the flavors of Persian cuisine, with many of the dishes being similar to what I grew up eating in Iraq. Ash reshteh is a unique herby soup usually made to celebrate Persian New Year (*Nowruz*), due to its abundance of herbs to welcome spring. The soup is full of legumes and leafy greens and seasoned with turmeric, and has a unique tangy flavor that comes from a Persian ingredient called *kashk*, which is liquid whey from fermented yogurt. It can be tricky to find, so sour cream and Greek yogurt are both great substitutes. The final touch is dollops of mint oil when serving. This soup is perfect to make if you need to use up herbs you have in your fridge.

1 In a large pot, heat the ¼ cup (60 ml) oil over medium-high heat for 1 minute. Add the onions and 1 teaspoon of the salt and cook, stirring often, for 10 minutes, or until softened and lightly golden. Stir in the garlic, mint, and turmeric and cook for another 30 seconds, or until the garlic is fragrant. Remove about one-quarter of this mixture and reserve to use as garnish.

2 Add the chickpeas, kidney beans, and lentils along with 10 cups (2.4 L) of water. Cover and cook over medium heat for 30 minutes, stirring occasionally, or until the lentils are tender.

3 Break the spaghetti in half and add it to the pot with the remaining 2 teaspoons salt. Cover and cook for 10 minutes over medium heat. Once the pasta is al dente, add the dill, parsley, cilantro, and spinach and cook for 5 to 7 minutes, until the herbs have wilted. Add the lemon juice, stir, and then taste and adjust for lemon juice and/or salt if necessary.

4 TO MAKE THE MINT OIL FOR GARNISH: Heat the 3 tablespoons oil in a small skillet over medium heat for 1 minute. Add the mint and stir for 20 seconds, or until it turns dark green. Remove from the heat.

5 Ladle into bowls and top with a bit of the reserved onion-garlic mixture, a few teaspoons of the mint oil, and a few large dollops of sour cream or yogurt.

Desserts & Drinks

Brown Butter Pistachio Basbousa SEMOLINA CAKE

YIELD: 26 to 30 pieces

PREP TIME: 15 minutes, plus 30 minutes cooling

COOK TIME: 35 minutes

◇◇◇◇◇

SIMPLE SYRUP

1½ cups (300 g) granulated sugar

Squeeze of fresh lemon juice

1 piece (1 inch, or 2.5 cm) lemon peel

BASBOUSA

⅔ cup (150 g) plus 1 tablespoon unsalted butter, divided

1½ cups (285 g) coarse semolina

1½ cups (285 g) medium or fine semolina

½ cup (45 g) packed unsweetened finely shredded coconut

¼ teaspoon salt

Grated zest of 2 lemons

⅔ cup (160 ml) whole milk

½ cup (120 ml) honey

¾ cup (150 g) granulated sugar

½ cup (85 g) roughly chopped unsalted pistachios (or substitute any other nuts)

This syrup-soaked semolina cake is one that is enjoyed in almost all countries in the Middle East and is often called different names, such as *namoura* in Lebanon, *hareesa* in Palestine, and *revani* in Turkey. Basbousa is the Egyptian name, and this particular recipe is Egyptian bakery–style: thinner and fudgy in texture. I've had a lot of basbousa in my lifetime, and many can verge on the sickly sweet and one-note end of the spectrum, or be quite dry in texture. But this recipe is none of those things. I use brown butter to add a delicious level of nuttiness that is further enhanced by the excessive amount of pistachios, which toast nicely in the oven as it bakes. There are two important steps to ensure you get this right: mixing the brown butter into the semolina to coat every grain until it's the texture of sand (this process is called *bas* in Arabic, which is likely how this dessert got its name) and making sure you use cooled syrup when pouring it over the hot basbousa to maintain a soft texture. Follow the steps in this recipe, and I promise I won't steer you wrong—but right into a possible basbousa overdose.

1 Preheat the oven to 400°F (205°F) and position a rack on the bottom.

2 **TO MAKE THE SIMPLE SYRUP:** In a small saucepan, combine the 1½ cups (300 g) sugar, lemon juice, and lemon peel with 1½ cups (300 ml) of water and bring to a boil over medium heat. Once boiling, reduce the heat to medium-low and let simmer for 10 minutes. Remove the pan from the heat and let cool.

3 **MEANWHILE, MAKE THE BASBOUSA:** Add ⅔ cup (160 g) of the butter to a small, light-colored saucepan over medium heat. Melt the butter, swirling the pan every few seconds. Once the butter is melted and starting to sizzle and foam around the edges, keep stirring with a silicone spatula to ensure it browns evenly. After about 5 minutes, the foam will slightly subside, the butter will turn golden brown, and the milk solids will look toasted. Immediately remove the pan from the heat and set aside.

4 In a large bowl, mix together the coarse semolina, medium or fine semolina, coconut, and salt. Add the lemon zest and mix well to combine.

CONTINUED ▶

5 Slowly add the brown butter to the semolina mixture, making sure to scrape the bottom of the pan to get all of the toasted milk solids in as well. Use a silicone spatula to mix the butter into the semolina, fully coating every grain; the mixture will look like crumbly wet sand.

6 In a medium microwave-safe glass bowl or measuring cup, combine the milk, honey, and ¾ cup (150 g) sugar and microwave on full power for 1 minute and 20 seconds. (If you don't have a microwave, simply heat the ingredients on the stovetop over medium heat until hot.) Whisk the wet ingredients together, then slowly pour over the dry ingredients, using the silicone spatula to combine the two. Do not overmix; stop when all the ingredients are visibly incorporated.

7 Grease a 12-inch (30 cm) round pan that is 1 inch (2.5 cm) deep with the remaining 1 tablespoon butter. (You may also use a rectangular pan.) Spoon the batter into the greased pan and use your hands to smooth it into an even layer. Sprinkle the chopped pistachios evenly over the surface.

8 Bake for 22 to 24 minutes, until the basbousa is firm to the touch. It's fine if the edges start to turn darker than the surface. Broil for 1 to 2 minutes to achieve a deeply golden color. Remove from the oven and immediately pour the cooled simple syrup evenly over the top (see Note); it will start to pool on the surface, so let it to sit for 30 minutes, or until all the syrup is absorbed and the basbousa has cooled.

9 Cut into small squares or diamonds and serve. Cover any leftovers with plastic wrap or place them in an airtight container and store on the counter for 4 to 5 days.

Note

It's important to ensure that the simple syrup is cool and that the basbousa is hot when the syrup is poured over it. If you use hot syrup, it will give the basbousa a hard texture.

Classic Walnut Baklawa

YIELD: 90 pieces

PREP TIME: 30 minutes, plus 1 hour cooling

COOK TIME: 55 minutes

◇◇◇◇◇

SIMPLE SYRUP

2½ cups (500 g) granulated sugar

Squeeze of fresh lemon juice

WALNUT FILLING

1½ pounds (700 g) unsalted whole raw walnuts (see Notes on page 220)

3 tablespoons ground cardamom

⅔ cup (135 g) granulated sugar

1 medium egg (see Notes on page 220)

PHYLLO PASTRY

½ cup (120 g) unsalted butter, melted

½ cup (120 g) olive oil

1 box (16 ounces, or 454 g) frozen phyllo dough (2 rolls; 18 sheets total), thawed for 1 hour

FOR GARNISHING

Crushed pistachios (optional)

Dried rose petals (optional)

I always think that I can have one piece of baklawa as a little sweet treat and then be done. But something just happens when you bite into it and immediately hear the crunch. I personally can never resist another piece—they're so small, after all. When I was thinking of including this recipe in this book, I wanted to get creative with my classic recipe, but my family would not hear of it. They demanded that I stick to this classic recipe and declared that it cannot be topped. Well, I listened to them. Baklawa (otherwise known as *baklava*) is an ancient dessert that can be traced back to the eighth century BCE, when people in the Assyrian Empire arranged unleavened flatbread in layers with nuts in between, though its exact origins are often debated. It is the main attraction at every Middle Eastern dessert spread. In Iraq, if you want to honor guests, you serve a large tray of baklawa. It comes in various shapes and can also be stuffed with pistachios or a thick cream filling. Store-bought baklawa is often too rich and too sweet, so I recommend making it yourself. I do have to give credit to my sister Sarra for perfecting the ingredient ratios in this family recipe: the cardamom-to-nuts ratio, the nuts-to-pastry ratio, and the syrup-to-baklawa ratio—everything has been perfected! And if you feel like it is too intimidating, trust me when I say that it is one of the easiest desserts to make.

1 Preheat the oven to 350°F (175°C).

2 TO MAKE THE SIMPLE SYRUP: In a medium saucepan, combine the sugar and lemon juice with 1¼ cups (300 ml) of water and bring to a boil over medium heat. Once boiling, reduce the heat to medium-low and let simmer for 10 minutes; it should have a runny, syrupy consistency. Remove the pan from the heat and let cool.

3 MEANWHILE, MAKE THE WALNUT FILLING: Add the walnuts to a food processor and grind until a coarse consistency; each walnut should break up to about a fifth of its size.

4 Transfer the ground walnuts to a medium bowl and add the cardamom, sugar, and egg. Mix well using a spoon.

5 TO PREPARE THE PHYLLO PASTRY: In a small bowl, combine the butter and oil.

CONTINUED ▶

6 Unwrap the phyllo dough package, unroll it, and cover the dough with a kitchen towel to prevent it from drying out while you work. Measure the sheets' dimensions against your pan (I used a 13 x 18-inch, or 33 x 46-cm, rimmed sheet pan) and snip any excess using scissors; the phyllo sheets should sit inside the pan up to the edges.

7 To assemble, generously brush the bottom of the pan with the butter-oil mixture, then layer 2 sheets of phyllo on top, ensuring you smooth them down and remove air bubbles as best you can every time you add a sheet. Brush the top sheet of phyllo generously with the butter-oil mixture, then continue layering 2 sheets at a time, brushing the top sheet with the butter-oil mixture, until you have 8 sheets (or half the phyllo dough) layered.

8 Spoon the walnut filling onto the phyllo pastry, covering it evenly and packing it down using the back of a spoon or your hand. Layer the remaining 8 phyllo sheets, brushing them with the butter-oil mixture, as you did in step 7.

9 Using a sharp knife, gently make straight cuts parallel to the long edge of the pan, roughly 1½ inches (4 cm) apart, all the way through to the bottom. Hold down the pastry gently as you cut and use a rocking motion so that the pastry does not get dragged out of place.

10 Make a diagonal cut from one corner of the pan, going all the way to the opposite corner, then make more diagonal cuts parallel to that, about 1 inch (2.5 cm) apart, to create diamond-shape pieces. Go over all the cuts twice to ensure you have cut through all the layers. (If it is easier, you can simply cut them into square shapes and adjust the size to your liking.)

11 Bake for 45 to 50 minutes, until the baklawa is a light golden color. Remove from the oven and immediately pour the cooled simple syrup over the top; you will hear a splashing sound as the cooled syrup hits the hot baklawa. Garnish with the crushed pistachios and rose petals (if using).

12 Let the baklawa cool for at least 1 hour in the pan before serving. If you plate it while hot, the baklawa will crumble.

Notes

+ You can substitute pistachios for the walnuts, or use a mixture of half each of walnuts and pistachios.

+ Using egg in the filling helps hold the filling together, especially when cutting the baklava. However, you can omit the egg if necessary for dietary restrictions.

+ Store leftovers in a container, uncovered, on the counter if you are consuming within a few days; otherwise, to maintain freshness, place in an airtight container and freeze. Thaw at room temperature for 1 hour before serving.

Samara's No-Bake Chocolate Biscuit Cake

YIELD: 8 to 10 servings

PREP TIME: 20 minutes, plus 4 hours chilling

◇◇◇◇◇◇

1 cup (240 g) unsalted butter

½ cup (100 g) granulated sugar

½ cup (50 g) unsweetened cocoa powder

1½ cups (360 ml) whole milk, divided

2 teaspoons instant coffee

12½ ounces (350 g) rectangular tea biscuits (see Notes)

FOR GARNISHING

½ cup (60 g) crushed pistachios

¼ cup (35 g) shaved or chopped chocolate of choice

Notes

+ You can use round biscuits if you can't find rectangular ones, but you may need to break them to fit the contours of the pan. I recommend specifically using tea biscuits or digestive biscuits, not any other type.

+ You can use any pan you have on hand and adjust the biscuits and chocolate sauce quantities to create at least 4 layers.

This recipe comes from my husband's cousin, my dear friend Samara. Whenever we get together and have family dinners, everyone knows that Samara will be bringing a large pan of this no-bake cold cake. And every time we enjoy it together, we discuss how she does everything "by eye" and how she tweaks it slightly every time she makes it, adding dark chocolate, adding more coffee, and using different biscuits. No matter what she does, it is always so delicious and gone in minutes. She exercised a lot of patience with me as we sent voice notes back and forth, her trying to be descriptive and me trying to be precise and capturing exact measurements.

1 In a medium saucepan, melt the butter over medium heat. Add the sugar and cocoa powder and whisk until combined, 4 to 5 minutes. Add 1 cup (240 ml) of the milk and continue to whisk for 5 minutes, or until the sauce starts to thicken and bubble. Remove the pan from the heat and whisk in the instant coffee until it is dissolved.

2 Line the bottom and sides of a loaf pan (see Notes) with plastic wrap, ensuring there is at least 2 inches (5 cm) of plastic wrap overhanging the sides of the pan (to act as "handles" when releasing the pan before serving).

3 Pour the remaining ½ cup (120 ml) milk into a small bowl. Start assembling the cake by dipping the tea biscuits in the milk for 1 second and arranging them on the bottom of the pan, side by side. Cover the biscuits with a layer of the chocolate sauce, ensuring all the biscuits are covered, then add another layer of biscuits dipped in milk, followed by another layer of chocolate sauce. Continue to layer the biscuits and chocolate sauce until the sauce is used up, with the top layer being chocolate sauce. You should have 5 or 6 biscuit layers if using a loaf pan.

4 Smooth the final layer of chocolate sauce using a butter knife. Cover the loaf pan with a separate piece of plastic wrap (not the overhanging plastic wrap) and refrigerate for at least 4 hours, or overnight.

5 Remove the top plastic wrap layer, and carefully use the overhanging plastic wrap to lift the cake out of the pan and onto a serving platter. The cake should be set enough to handle.

6 Garnish with the crushed pistachios and shaved chocolate, then slice and serve.

Om Mahmoud's Ka'ak Simsim
SESAME COOKIES

YIELD: 25 cookies
PREP TIME 30 minutes
COOK TIME: 20 minutes

⬦⬦⬦⬦⬦

1¾ cups (210 g) all-purpose flour

1 cup (200 g) granulated sugar

1 tablespoon baking powder

2 teaspoons ground cardamom

2 medium eggs

1 cup (240 g) unsalted butter, melted

1½ cups (225 g) white sesame seeds

Ka'ak are Iraqi cookies commonly served for guests at teatime. When I was writing this book, my sister Heba was a newlywed. That's when Khala Om Mahmoud entered our lives (as my sister's mother-in-law), and when we first tasted her delicious ka'ak simsim. Every time she would visit us or we would visit her, without fail, there would be a large platter of these cookies. And without fail, we would pour a cup of chai, then grab one. Then another. And another. When she sent me her recipe, I was so surprised at how simple they were to make, only requiring a few ingredients. These are the perfect tea cookies, slightly crispy, with a delicious depth of flavor from the sesame and a beautiful hint of cardamom.

1 Preheat the oven to 350°F (175°C). Line a large sheet pan with parchment paper.

2 In a large bowl, combine the flour, sugar, baking powder, and cardamom and mix until well incorporated.

3 Whisk the eggs in a small bowl, then add them to the dry ingredients along with the melted butter. Mix the wet ingredients into the dry ingredients, either using your hands or a stand mixer, until a thick cookie dough forms.

4 Cover the bowl with plastic wrap and place in the refrigerator for 10 minutes.

5 Place the sesame seeds in a shallow bowl or plate. Scoop about 1 tablespoon of the cookie dough. Roll it into a thin rope, roughly 4 inches (10 cm) in length and ½ inch (1.3 cm) in width, then twist the rope into a circular shape, sticking the ends together (see Note). Dip it into the sesame seeds, covering one side of the cookie, then place it on the prepared sheet pan, seeds side up. Repeat with the remaining dough, placing them 1 inch (2.5 cm) apart and baking in batches.

6 Bake for 15 minutes, or until the cookies are lightly golden and set. Broil for 2 to 3 minutes, until the tops are golden.

Note
Shape the cookies into thin ropes, because they will spread in the oven. If you make the ropes too thick, they will lose their circular shape.

Aish El Saraya
BREAD PUDDING

YIELD: 6 servings

PREP TIME: 20 minutes, plus 2 hours chilling

◇◇◇◇◇

BREAD PUDDING

1½ cups (300 g) granulated sugar
Squeeze of fresh lemon juice
6 slices brioche bread

ASHTA

2 cups (473 ml) heavy whipping cream
2 cups (473 ml) whole milk
½ cup (100 g) granulated sugar
½ cup (60 g) cornstarch
2 teaspoons rose water

FOR GARNISHING

¼ cup (30 g) crushed pistachios
2 tablespoons dried rosebuds (optional)

The name of this dessert translates to "palace bread" because of its decadence and beauty—it is often decorated with bright green pistachios and dried rosebuds. It consists of a layer of buttery bread soaked in syrup, topped with a rich *ashta*, which is a thickened cream. Any white bread can be used in this recipe, but my favorite bread to use is brioche, for an extra-rich flavor. It is a cold dessert, often served at celebrations or during Ramadan. It is usually made in a large dish, but individual servings are also a beautiful way to present it.

1 TO MAKE THE BREAD PUDDING: Preheat the oven to 400°F (205°C).

2 In a small saucepan, combine the sugar and lemon juice with 1 cup (240 ml) of water for a simple syrup, and bring to a boil over medium heat. Once boiling, reduce the heat to medium-low and let simmer for 10 minutes. Remove the saucepan from the heat and let cool to room temperature.

3 MEANWHILE, MAKE THE ASHTA: In a medium saucepan, combine the cream, milk, sugar, and cornstarch and whisk until the cornstarch is dissolved. Place the pot over medium heat and cook for 10 minutes, whisking continuously, until the ashta thickens. Stir in the rose water, remove from the heat, and let cool.

4 Place the brioche slices on a large sheet pan and toast in the oven for 5 to 7 minutes, flipping halfway through, until golden. Let cool.

5 In a food processor, add the toasted brioche, a few slices at a time, and process to a fine consistency. Transfer the bread crumbs to a large bowl, then add ¾ cup (180 ml) of the simple syrup and mix to combine (reserve the remaining simple syrup for serving) into a wet, crumbly mixture.

6 Spoon 2 to 3 tablespoons of the bread crumbs into the base of each of 6 small parfait serving cups and pack them down. If using one baking dish, use a 9-inch (23 cm) square pan. Layer about ½ cup (120 ml) of ashta on top of the bread layer in each cup and smooth it out. Cover each serving cup with plastic wrap, making sure that the plastic is in contact with the ashta layer to help prevent a film from forming on the surface. Place in the refrigerator for at least 2 hours, or overnight.

7 When ready to serve, remove the plastic wrap, garnish with the crushed pistachios and rosebuds (if using), and serve with the remaining simple syrup.

Moroccan Ghriba
ALMOND COOKIES

YIELD: 20 cookies
PREP TIME: 20 minutes
COOK TIME: 15 minutes

◇◇◇◇◇

10½ ounces (300 g) blanched almond flour

½ teaspoon baking powder

⅔ cup (135 g) granulated sugar

Grated zest of 2 lemons

3 tablespoons unsalted butter, softened

2 medium egg yolks

¼ cup (60 ml) plus 1 teaspoon orange blossom water, divided

1 teaspoon almond extract (optional)

1 cup (120 g) powdered sugar

Note

Store the cookies in an airtight container on the counter for up to 1 week.

Moroccans serve an assortment of traditional cookies during celebrations like Eid, referred to as *ghriba* cookies. There are various types of ghriba: coconut, almond, pistachio, and rose-scented, among many others. They can be made with all-purpose flour or semolina, but this version uses only almond flour. The best part about this cookie is the crispiness on the outside and the chewiness on the inside, coupled with the hint of lemon. They are absolutely addictive. When my dad tasted one of my test batches, he immediately asked my mom to make a double batch and stash it in their freezer. They are one of the simplest cookies to make—just make sure you do not overbake them! Stick to the timing in this recipe, and they'll be perfect.

1 Preheat the oven to 350°F (175°C) and position a rack on the bottom.

2 In a large bowl, mix together the almond flour and baking powder.

3 In a medium bowl, combine the sugar and lemon zest and use your hands to rub the zest into the sugar to extract the flavor. Add the almond flour to the bowl and whisk until the ingredients are well combined.

4 Add the butter and egg yolks to the dry ingredients and use your hands to work them in until a crumbly mixture forms; you should be able to form a ball when squeezing the mixture together. Add 1 teaspoon of the orange blossom water and the almond extract (if using) and mix well.

5 Place the powdered sugar in a small bowl and the remaining ¼ cup (60 ml) orange blossom water in a separate small bowl. Line two medium baking sheets with parchment paper, or use one baking sheet and bake the cookies in batches.

6 Scoop ¾ tablespoon of cookie dough. Dip your hands in the orange blossom water to wet your hands and roll the dough into a ball. Gently flatten the ball very slightly, then roll it in the powdered sugar until completely covered. Place on a prepared baking sheet, 1 inch (2.5 cm) apart. Repeat with the remaining dough, wetting your hands with the orange blossom water as you shape each cookie.

7 Bake on the bottom rack for 15 minutes; the cookies will start to develop cracks, which is normal. Do not overbake, even if they still seem soft; they will firm up as they cool. Cool on the baking sheet for 10 minutes before serving.

Mini Cheese Kunafa

SHREDDED PHYLLO STUFFED WITH CHEESE

YIELD: 12 servings

PREP TIME: 15 minutes

COOK TIME: 45 minutes

◇◇◇◇◇

SIMPLE SYRUP

2½ cups (300 g) granulated sugar

Squeeze of fresh lemon juice

1 tablespoon rose or orange blossom water (optional)

KUNAFA

1⅓ pounds (600 g) high-moisture mozzarella cheese, shredded or cut into small cubes

¾ cup (180 ml) canned thick table cream

1 box (16 ounces, or 454 g) frozen kataifi dough (shredded phyllo dough), thawed for 1 hour

1 cup (240 ml) unsalted butter, melted, plus 2 tablespoons for greasing

FOR GARNISHING

½ cup (60 g) crushed pistachios

2 tablespoons dried rose petals (optional)

I'm confident enough to declare that kunafa (also pronounced *knafa*, or *knafeh*) is my favorite dessert of all time. It's the combination of crispy, shredded dough drenched in syrup, plus warm, melty cheese that is absolutely magical. This is another crown jewel on the Middle Eastern dessert table. Its origins are not precisely known, but it may be traced back to Palestine, Syria, or Egypt in its earliest forms. It's traditionally made with shredded phyllo dough that's been generously rubbed with butter or ghee, then layered with sweet cheese, thick cream, or nuts, with the cheese version being the most popular. It's made in very large circular trays, then, when fresh out of the oven while the cheese is still warm, drenched in sugar syrup and sprinkled with crushed pistachios. The dough can be one of two different varieties: *khishna* (meaning "rough") or *na'ama* (meaning "soft"). Kunafa khishna is made with shredded phyllo dough; kunafa na'ama is specific to the region of Nablus, Palestine, and it's made with a crumbly semolina and flour–based dough. The recipe I come back to time and again is this simple cheese kunafa stuffed with mozzarella cheese. That's right: this recipe does not require you to go hunting for the specific sweet cheese used in the Middle East. I find high-moisture mozzarella to have just enough salt to create a lovely balance with the sweet syrup. I also love making it into mini servings using a muffin pan, but this recipe can also easily be made in a large, circular tray.

1 Preheat the oven to 350°F (175°C).

2 **TO MAKE THE SIMPLE SYRUP:** In a medium saucepan, combine the sugar and lemon juice with 1¼ cups (300 ml) of water and bring to a boil over high heat. Once boiling, reduce the heat to medium and let simmer for 10 minutes. Remove from the heat, stir in the rose or orange water blossom (if using), and let cool to room temperature.

3 **MEANWHILE, MAKE THE KUNAFAS:** In a medium bowl, mix together the mozzarella and cream.

4 Break up the kataifi dough using your hands and place it in a food processor. Process for a few seconds until it is broken up into small pieces, at least ¼ inch (6 mm) long. Alternatively, you can shred it on a cutting board using a sharp knife.

CONTINUED ▶

5 Transfer the shredded kataifi dough to a large bowl and pour the melted butter over it. Using your hands, massage the butter into the dough, making sure to saturate every strand.

6 Brush the bottoms and sides of a 12-cup muffin pan with butter. Spoon the kataifi into the muffin cups, filling each one about halfway. Using your fingers, flatten the kataifi onto the bottom of each muffin cup, allowing the pastry to also line the edges, creating a small cup shape. Spoon about 1½ tablespoons of the cheese mixture into each muffin cup. Take the remaining kataifi dough and spread it over the cheese, completely covering it and tightly packing it in.

7 Bake for 40 to 45 minutes, until the outside is deeply golden and crispy. Remove from the oven and carefully flip the muffin tray over onto a large sheet pan to release all the mini kunafas. Immediately drizzle the mini kunafas with most of the simple syrup, covering the entire surface of each one. Reserve a bit of simple syrup for serving.

8 Garnish with the crushed pistachios and rose petals (if using). Serve on small plates or a large platter with simple syrup on the side.

Iraqi Churag
SWEET BUNS

YIELD: 25 to 30 buns

PREP TIME: 1 hour, plus 1 hour rising

COOK TIME: 25 minutes

◇◇◇◇◇

4 cups plus 3 tablespoons (500 g) all-purpose flour

½ teaspoon kosher salt

¾ cup (180 ml) warm water

½ cup (120 ml) warm whole milk (microwave for 30 seconds)

½ tablespoon instant yeast

¼ cup (50 g) granulated sugar

2 large eggs, separated

½ cup (120 ml) olive oil, plus more for greasing

⅓ cup (50 g) white sesame seeds

1 cup (240 ml) honey

Churag is one of Iraq's most iconic pastries, sold at all bakeries and by local street vendors. It's a sweet bread topped with honey and sesame seeds and served with a cup of tea as an afternoon snack. The dough contains egg yolks, so it's similar to brioche in texture. I've made many different types of dough before, and this is one of the easiest. It will rise into a very soft dough that's easy to work with, and once baked, it will have a fluffy cloudlike texture. The traditional shape is that of a twisted braid shaped into a flower. It is often kept plain and drizzled with honey after baking or stuffed with dates. You can also make a savory version by brushing it with an herb butter after baking or stuffing it with cheese.

1 In a large bowl, mix together the flour and salt.

2 In a medium bowl, whisk together the warm water, warm milk, and yeast until the yeast is dissolved. Add the sugar, egg yolks, and oil and whisk to combine.

3 Slowly add the wet ingredients to the flour and mix the dough using your hands until it comes together; at first the dough will feel wet, but start kneading it on the counter for 5 to 7 minutes, until it comes together and has a smooth and soft texture. Cover the bowl with plastic wrap and a kitchen towel and let the dough rise for 1 hour, or until it doubles in size.

4 While the dough rises, place the sesame seeds in a medium dry skillet over medium-low heat. Stir continuously for 4 to 5 minutes, or until the sesame seeds are slightly darker in color and fragrant. Remove and set aside to cool.

5 When the dough is ready, preheat the oven to 350°F (175°C). Line two large baking sheets with parchment paper.

6 Divide the dough into small balls, roughly 40 to 50 grams in weight. Lay the dough balls on a large tray and cover loosely with plastic wrap to prevent them from drying out while you shape the churag.

7 Place the sesame seeds in a shallow bowl or plate. Beat the egg whites in a small bowl.

CONTINUED ▶

8 On a lightly oiled surface, roll a dough ball into a rope 10 to 12 inches (25 to 30 cm) long, using even pressure so that the rope is the same width from end to end. Cut the rope in half to form 2 ropes, then arrange the ropes side by side and pinch them together at one end. Braid the rope by bringing the right one over the left one, then the left over the right, and so on. Bring the ends together to create a circular braid and pinch them to seal. Gently tuck the pinched end underneath for a clean look. Lightly brush the top of the churag with egg whites, then dip the top in the toasted sesame seeds and place on a prepared baking sheet. Repeat with the remaining dough balls, placing them 1 inch (2.5 cm) apart since they will double in size.

9 Bake for 20 to 25 minutes, until the bottoms are lightly golden. Broil for a few minutes until the tops are lightly golden. Remove from the oven and lightly brush each bun with some honey while warm to achieve a shiny surface.

10 Place the churag on a platter and cover with plastic wrap or a towel to keep them moist. Serve warm or at room temperature.

Note

You can freeze the churag in an airtight freezer bag or container for 2 to 3 months after baking them, then reheat in the oven to enjoy warm. Also, if you struggle to shape them as described, you can simply shape each ball into a long thin rope, then twist it onto itself to create a pinwheel shape.

Orange Cake

YIELD: 10 to 12 servings

PREP TIME: 15 minutes

COOK TIME: 45 minutes

◇◇◇◇◇

1 cup (240 ml) plus 1 tablespoon
vegetable oil, divided

2 cups (240 g) plus 1 tablespoon
all-purpose flour, divided

3 large oranges

2 teaspoons baking powder

½ teaspoon kosher salt

1 cup (200 g) granulated sugar

3 teaspoons ground cardamom
(optional)

3 eggs, at room temperature

FOR GARNISHING

1 tablespoon powdered sugar

This simple orange cake was tested six times before I was happy with the results. I was adamant about including a cake that was unfussy and perfectly delicious on its own—no need for any glaze or icing! I also don't particularly enjoy baking, so the only cake I'll bake is one that I can mix in a bowl using a whisk or spatula. I don't want many steps, I don't want to wait for anything to chill, and I don't want to take out my stand mixer. This orange cake is the answer. It reminds me of the cakes we used to always have at the breakfast table or at teatime. We would often cut a slice of cake and top it with plain yogurt to enjoy. I recently asked a few Iraqi friends if they did this as well and was met with blank stares. Maybe it was just our family. But make this cake and try it! I do have to warn you though: zesting the oranges is a bit of a workout, so feel free to get someone else involved and pass it on to them while you do the "hard" part.

1 Preheat the oven to 350°F (175°C) and position the rack in the middle. Grease a 10-cup (2.4 L) Bundt pan with 1 tablespoon of the oil, then dust it with 1 tablespoon of the flour. Tap the outside of the pan to circulate the flour so that it covers the inside surface.

2 Zest the oranges (avoiding the white pith) into a small bowl to yield roughly 4 to 5 tablespoons of orange zest. Juice the oranges into a separate small bowl to yield ¾ cup (180 ml) of juice.

3 In a large bowl, whisk together the remaining 2 cups (240 g) flour, the baking powder, salt, granulated sugar, and cardamom (if using). Whisk in the orange zest.

4 In a medium bowl, whisk the remaining 1 cup (240 ml) oil, the eggs, and orange juice until combined.

5 Gradually fold the wet ingredients into the dry ingredients using a silicone spatula until the wet and dry ingredients are just combined and you no longer see flour streaks. Do not overmix the batter. Pour the batter into the prepared Bundt pan.

6 Bake for 45 minutes, or until a toothpick inserted into the center comes out clean. Let cool for 10 minutes, then carefully flip onto a cake plate or stand. Let cool completely.

7 Dust with the powdered sugar, slice, and serve.

Turkish Sutlaç with Mastic
RICE PUDDING

YIELD: 8 to 10 small servings

PREP TIME: 5 minutes

COOK TIME: 40 minutes

◇◇◇◇◇

6 cups (1.5 L) whole milk

¾ cup (180 ml) cold heavy whipping cream

1½ tablespoons cornstarch

¼ teaspoon mastic gum (see Notes; optional)

¾ cup (170 g) short-grain rice, rinsed until the water runs clear and drained completely

1 cup (200 g) granulated sugar

Notes

+ If you don't have mastic gum, you can choose any other flavoring for the pudding, such as vanilla, cardamom, rose water, or orange blossom water. Simply add 1 to 2 teaspoons of any of these options after the pudding is cooked and just before broiling.

+ Store leftovers in the refrigerator covered with plastic wrap for 4 to 5 days.

Rice pudding is one of those desserts that spans many cultures and countries, with each region having its own variation. One of the most impressive presentations is that of sutlaç, which is the Turkish version. It is traditionally cooked on the stovetop, then broiled for a few minutes to develop a beautifully browned and spotty top layer due to the caramelization of the milk. It's served in individual ramekins, usually cold, but you can also serve it warm out of the oven (which is actually how I prefer it). You can flavor the pudding with vanilla, cardamom, cinnamon, rose water, or anything you prefer. But my favorite is definitely a small pinch of crushed mastic gum. If you can find it at a local Middle Eastern store, you must try it.

1 Add the milk to a medium saucepan and heat over medium heat until hot but not boiling. Remove from the heat.

2 In a small bowl, combine the cream and cornstarch and mix until the cornstarch has dissolved. Using a mortar and pestle, crush the mastic gum (if using) into a fine powder.

3 Add the rice to a large pan or skillet at least 2 inches (5 cm) deep. Add 2 ladles of the hot milk and gently simmer together over medium heat, stirring constantly. When the rice has absorbed most of the milk, add a few more ladles of hot milk and continue to stir until most of the milk is absorbed. Continue adding milk, a few ladles at a time, stirring until most of it is absorbed. (This method is similar to how you would cook a risotto; while slow, this process will yield very creamy results.) Once you have used all the milk, add the sugar and stir for a few minutes until it is dissolved. Add the whipping cream–cornstarch mixture and continue to stir until the pudding is thickened and the rice is cooked to a very soft consistency. This process should take 30 to 40 minutes in total.

4 Stir in the mastic gum powder (if using) or other flavoring (see Notes). Remove the pan from the heat. Pour the rice pudding into oven-safe 5- to 6-ounce (150 to 180 ml) ramekins for individual servings, arranging them on a large sheet pan. Turn on the oven broiler and place the sheet pan directly under the broiler. Broil for 1 to 2 minutes (at the most), until the surfaces are caramelized and look spotty and browned. Remove and let cool for a few minutes.

5 Serve warm (my favorite), at room temperature, or cover with plastic wrap, refrigerate for 2 hours, and then serve cold.

Egyptian Karkade
HIBISCUS ICED TEA

YIELD: 6 servings

PREP TIME: 5 minutes, plus 2 hours chilling

COOK TIME: 5 minutes

◇◇◇◇◇

6 cups (1.4 L) filtered water
1 cup (33 g) dried hibiscus flowers
½ cup (100 g) granulated sugar
   (or more per preference)

FOR GARNISHING AND SERVING
Ice cubes (optional)
Fresh mint leaves

When you're in Egypt and you think of iced tea, you won't find the familiar North American version using black tea. Instead, you'll find this bright pink hibiscus iced tea, with a tart and fruity flavor somewhat resembling cranberries. It's said to have been the preferred drink of the pharaohs. I'm not quite sure how it made its way to Iraq, but I grew up drinking karkade regularly, especially during Ramadan. It's served ice cold and usually sweetened with sugar to balance the tartness. It's important to use high-quality dried hibiscus petals to get optimal flavor. It's easy to make ahead and beautiful to serve to guests, garnished with fresh mint leaves. Just be careful you don't get any of it on your countertops—it can easily stain them!

1 Add the filtered water to a medium saucepan and bring to a boil.

2 Add the hibiscus flowers and sugar. Let boil for 5 minutes until the sugar is dissolved. Turn off the heat and allow the hibiscus to steep in the water for 20 minutes. You may taste and adjust for more sugar at this point. To add more, stir it into the tea while it is still hot until it dissolves.

3 Strain the tea into a pitcher, being careful not to spill any on easily stained counters (the hibiscus is highly pigmented).

4 Refrigerate for at least 2 hours. If the tea is too strong, feel free to dilute it with more cold water, but do not dilute too much if serving with ice cubes.

5 Serve with ice cubes (if using) and garnish with mint leaves.

Laymoon W Na'ana
MINT LEMONADE

YIELD: 5 servings

PREP TIME: 10 minutes

◇◇◇◇◇

1¼ cups (300 ml) fresh lemon juice
  (8 to 10 large lemons)

¾ cup (150 g) granulated sugar
  (or less, per preference)

2 cups (100 g) loosely packed fresh
  mint leaves

2½ cups (600 ml) filtered water

2 cups ice cubes

FOR GARNISHING

Fresh mint leaves

Mint lemonade needs no introduction or explanation; it's simply one of the most refreshing drinks on a hot summer day. It is served at every restaurant in the Middle East, sometimes in a completely liquified form and sometimes like a frozen slushie. You can vary the amount of sugar based on your preference and serve it garnished with beautiful fresh mint leaves.

1 Add the lemon juice, sugar, mint leaves, and water to a large high-powered blender and blend for 1 to 2 minutes, until the sugar is dissolved.

2 Add the ice and blend again for a few seconds, or until the ice is crushed.

3 Pour into drinking glasses and garnish with mint leaves.

Baba's Black Grapes & Mint Juice

YIELD: 4 to 6 servings

PREP TIME: 10 minutes

◇◇◇◇◇

4 cups (400 g) seedless black grapes, plus more to taste

1½ cups (360 ml) filtered water

¾ cup (40 g) packed fresh mint leaves

1 cup ice cubes

FOR GARNISHING AND SERVING

Ice cubes (optional)

Fresh mint leaves

In Mosul, a city in northern Iraq where I was born, *sharbat zbeeb* is a very popular drink, made from plump black raisins and fragrant dried mint. The process is lengthy, usually requiring soaking of both the raisins and the mint for at least a day. My dad grew up with this drink, so he developed his own (very similar) version using fresh black grapes and fresh mint, simply blitzing them in a blender. He makes this drink for us often, especially during Ramadan. My kids absolutely love it. It needs no added sugar due to the natural sweetness of the grapes. He runs the blended juice through a fine-mesh strainer to get rid of all the grape peel bits. Black grapes are the preferred type for this drink due to their deeper flavor, but you can easily use purple grapes, since black ones are harder to find.

1 Add the grapes, water, and mint leaves to a high-powered blender and blend for a few seconds, or until the ingredients are juiced.

2 Add 1 cup ice cubes and blend for a few more seconds. Taste and adjust; if it is too watery, add more grapes and blend again.

3 Place a fine-mesh strainer over a large bowl or jug and pour the juice through it to strain out the large bits of grape skin.

4 Pour the strained juice into a pitcher and either refrigerate or serve immediately over more ice cubes. Garnish with fresh mint leaves.

Turkish Coffee

YIELD: 4 servings (Turkish coffee cups)
PREP TIME: 10 minutes

◇◇◇◇◇

5 tablespoons Turkish coffee (finely
  ground coffee)

1 to 2 tablespoons granulated sugar
  (See Note)

FOR SERVING

Turkish delight, cookies, chocolates,
  or sweet treat of choice

Although this is Turkish-style coffee, it has been part of Arabic culture and tradition for thousands of years. Every single Arab home you visit will surely offer you a *finjan qahwa* with dessert. A *finjan* is the cup that it is served in. Turkish coffee is traditionally made using a Turkish *cezve* or, in Arabic, a *dalla*, which is a small, long-handled pot with a spout. The strong, finely ground coffee is stirred with water for a few minutes, then left to brew until boiling. But you must stand near it because it happens quickly; I still recall having to stand over the stove and make the coffee for guests when I was little, many times forgetting to watch it and letting it spill all over the stove. Once it boils, foam will form on the surface, which is what we call the "face" of the coffee and makes each finjan look beautiful. This foam is spooned into all the finjans equally, then the coffee is poured on top. It's most commonly flavored with cardamom, although you'll also find varieties with mastic or hazelnut.

1 Add the coffee and sugar to a Turkish coffeepot.

2 Using a small Turkish coffee cup, measure out 5 cups (1.2 L) of filtered water and add it to the coffeepot.

3 Place the coffeepot over medium heat and stir for a minute to dissolve the coffee and sugar. Let the coffee come to a boil, 4 to 5 minutes. As soon as the coffee starts to boil, remove the pot from the heat. A layer of coffee foam will form at the top of the pot. Using a teaspoon, scoop the foam into each coffee cup, then pour the coffee. Each cup will have a small layer of foam. The bottom of the coffee will have a thick layer of coffee grounds which you leave in the pot (but it's fine if some of it gets into the cup).

4 Serve with Turkish delight, cookies, chocolates, or any other sweet treat.

Note

Turkish coffee is strong and hence it is always served per preference with regards to sweetness. There are three common sweetness levels: no sugar, medium, or sweet. Typically, the medium level requires 1 tablespoon of sugar per 1 tablespoon of coffee. The sweet level requires 2 tablespoons of sugar per 1 tablespoon of coffee.

Chai Bi Na'ana
MINT BLACK TEA

YIELD: 6 servings (4-ounce, or 120-ml, chai cups)

COOK TIME: 10 minutes

◇◇◇◇◇

3 cups (720 ml) filtered water

4 tablespoons loose-leaf black tea

1 cup (50 g) loosely packed fresh mint leaves

FOR SERVING

Granulated sugar

In Iraq, and I'm sure this goes for other Arab countries, chai is almost always prepared before we eat dinner, so it is piping hot and ready to pour into teacups as soon as we're finished eating. No one likes to wait around for tea; it must be served immediately! Black tea is the preferred choice across the Middle East, almost always flavored with mint or cardamom (but never both!). It is poured into an *istikan* (what we call the little teacups in Iraq), along with sugar per preference (make mine sweet, please!). Usually, a second pot of boiled water is served along with the teapot and is used to dilute the tea for those who like theirs weaker.

1 Add the water to a stovetop teapot (or a saucepan) with a strainer then add the loose-leaf tea to the strainer. Place the teapot over medium-high heat and bring to a boil.

2 Once boiling, reduce the heat to medium-low and let simmer for 5 minutes. After 5 minutes, and after you smell the tea strongly, turn off the heat.

3 Boil a kettle of water to serve on the side. The water can be used to reduce the strength of the tea for those who like it less strong.

4 Place some of the mint leaves in each teacup, then pour the tea into the teacups.

5 Serve with sugar for sweetening.

Karak Chai

SPICED TEA WITH MILK

YIELD: 6 servings (4-ounce, or 120-ml, chai cups)

COOK TIME: 10 minutes

◇◇◇◇◇

6 green cardamom pods

5 whole cloves

3 cups (720 ml) filtered water

2 cinnamon sticks

3 tablespoons loose-leaf black tea

½ cup (120 ml) evaporated milk

¼ cup (50 g) granulated sugar, or to taste

FOR SERVING

Tea biscuits

Karak chai was popularized in the Middle East, especially in the Persian Gulf, due to the vast influence of South Asians in the region. My husband's family lives in Kuwait, and when we visit, we often find little roadside shops selling this spiced milk tea, piping hot and with a delicious aroma. It's so comforting, especially in the colder months, and you can adjust the whole spices to your taste. My family and I always make this when we are all gathered together and want a little something special to drink, aside from our regular black tea. The most important thing is not to forget the tea biscuits for dunking!

1 Place the cardamom pods and cloves in a mortar and crush them lightly to break open the cardamom pods and crush the cloves into smaller pieces.

2 In a medium saucepan, combine the water, cinnamon sticks, crushed cloves, and cardamom pods. Place the saucepan over medium-high heat and bring to a boil.

3 Once boiling, add the loose-leaf black tea, reduce the heat to medium-low, and let simmer for 2 to 3 minutes. Add the evaporated milk and sugar and bring the chai to a boil over high heat. Remove the saucepan from the heat until the bubbles stop, then place it back over high heat for a second boil. Once it bubbles again, reduce the heat to medium-low and let simmer for 5 minutes or longer, depending on your preferred tea strength.

4 Turn off the heat and pour into chai cups through a tea strainer. Serve with tea biscuits.

Note

You may skip adding the sugar to the saucepan and, instead, add sugar when serving into cups per preference.

ACKNOWLEDGMENTS

The Hungry Paprikas online community: Thank you for trusting me with your groceries, for allowing me into your homes through my recipes, and for always supporting my work. I am grateful to be on this journey with you.

Mama: There are no words to describe the true extent of how thankful I am that you are my mother. Thank you for teaching me love, kindness, leadership, resilience, and gratitude.

Baba: Thank you for the sacrifices you made to provide my sisters and I with the best life we can ask for. I love you.

Omar: Everyone thinks you are lucky to eat the food I cook every day. But they don't know that I am the lucky one. Thank you for always being right next to me.

Zayd and Joud: My life would be dull indeed without your laughter in it. Thank you for being the light of my life, and the beat of my heart. I love you, always.

Sarra: Thank you for being my rock, and my trusted confidante. I'm not sure what I would do without you, or where to begin with thanking you.

Heba: The little sister I can always count on when I want to have a good time, and the one always willing to be a taste tester. Thank you for supporting me, always.

My extended family (my in-laws, aunts and uncles, nieces, and nephews): Your support and encouragement mean so much to me. Thank you for always giving me a sense of belonging. I love you all.

Lynn: Only you would still listen to my long-winded voice notes after fourteen years of long-distance friendship. Thank you for being my best friend.

Zeena: You've watched me through every stage of this cookbook journey and listened to me patiently through it all. I'm so thankful for our friendship.

My friends and board of advisors (Sarah, Zahra, Nadia, Doaa, Rawan, and Kathryn): There's nothing like a group of girlfriends who get what you do. The ones who expect to receive a text from me at odd hours of the night, and the ones who always set me right. Thank you for always being there.

Humaira: I couldn't have asked for a better team member, and a better friend. Thank you for your cooking, testing, advising, and moral support.

My recipe testers: Razan, Hafsa, Linda, Safia, Sonia, Hala, Hilary, Malaka, Mariam, Manar, Zoha, Fatima, Sana, Alicia, Sara, Manal, Mowa, Nadira, Zeinab, Rashida, Ayah, Inge, Patti, Christopher, Liza, Sally, Lisa, and Fareen. Thank you for your time and thorough feedback. You made this journey so much more fun, and I appreciate your support and dedication to the success of my cookbook.

Erin: Thank you for choosing me and believing in me. And for being the best editor a girl can ask for.

The Quarto team: You brought my book to life with your talent and skills. Thank you for everything you do.

INDEX